ACHIEVING EDUCATIONAL JUSTICE: A NARRATIVE OF CRUSADE FOR REFORMATION

A NARRATIVE OF CRUSADE FOR REFORMATION

APURV PANDEY

सत्यं ब्रूयात् प्रियं ब्रूयात् , न ब्रूयात् सत्यम् अप्रियम् ।

प्रियं च नानृतम् ब्रूयात् , एष धर्मः सनातनः ॥

❦❦❦

Contents

Disclaimer

The stories and accounts presented in this book are based on real events and experiences, but some names and identifying details have been changed to protect the privacy of the individuals involved. The views and opinions expressed in this book are those of the author and do not necessarily reflect the views of the individuals featured or the organizations they are affiliated with. The author and publisher of this book do not endorse or condone any acts of cruelty or violence described in the book. The purpose of this book is to raise awareness about the harsh realities of the world and to inspire change and understanding. The author and publisher of this book will not be liable for any errors or omissions in the information provided or for any actions taken based on the information provided.

<h1 style="text-align:center">Foreword</h1>

It is my honor to write the foreword for "Achieving Educational Justice: A Narrative of Crusade for Reformation," written by the young and incredibly talented author, Apurv Pandey. This book is a powerful testament to the determination and passion of one young person to make a difference in the world.

Apurv's story, as told in this book, is one of a child who, at a young age, became aware of the inequalities and injustices present in the education system. Rather than accepting these inequalities as the status quo, Apurv chose to take action and do something about it. Through extensive research and personal anecdotes, Apurv has written a compelling and thought-provoking book that highlights the need for educational reform and offers practical solutions for achieving educational justice for all students.

What is most striking about this book is that it was written by a child. Apurv's unique perspective and voice give the book a sense of urgency and realism that only someone who has experienced the challenges of the education system first-hand can bring. His ability to express such complex ideas in a clear and concise manner is truly impressive, and serves as a reminder that young people have the power to effect change in the world.

I believe that this book will inspire others to join the crusade for educational justice and will serve as a valuable resource for educators, policymakers, and anyone interested in creating a more just and equitable society. I encourage all readers to take the time to read this book and consider the ideas presented within. Apurv Pandey's Achieving Educational Justice is an important contribution to the ongoing discussion about how to create a more equitable and just education system for all students.

It is also important to note that Apurv's book is not just about the problems faced by marginalized students in the education system, but it also delves into the solutions that have been implemented by educators and advocates and the ones that can be done to make the education system more just and fair. Apurv's perspective as a student, combined with his research and analysis, provides valuable insights into the ways in which educators, policymakers, and communities can work together to create a more inclusive and equitable education system.

Throughout the book, Apurv highlights the importance of listening to the voices and experiences of marginalized students and their families, and the need to empower them in the fight for educational justice. He stresses the importance of understanding the systemic issues that perpetuate educational disparities and how to address them. The solutions Apurv puts forward in the book are practical and feasible, and he makes a convincing case for why it is necessary to take action to reform the education system.

In conclusion, I cannot stress enough the importance of this book, particularly in a time where issues of equity and social justice are at the forefront of the national discourse. I believe that Achieving Educational Justice: A Narrative of Crusade for Reformation is a must-read for anyone who cares about creating a more just and equitable society. Apurv Pandey is a young author with a powerful voice and a message that should be heard by all. I am proud to have had the opportunity to write the foreword for this important book, and I hope that it will inspire many to join the crusade for educational justice.

Furthermore, Apurv's book also delves into the potential long-term impacts of educational injustice, both on individual students and on society as a whole. He illustrates how the lack of access to quality education for certain groups of students not only affects their immediate academic and career prospects, but also perpetuates systemic inequalities and societal issues such as poverty and inequality.

One of the most powerful aspects of the book is that it is a call to action. Apurv encourages readers to take responsibility for the education system and to actively work towards change. He emphasizes that achieving educational justice is not something that can be achieved overnight, but rather it is an ongoing process that requires the involvement and commitment of everyone, particularly educators, policymakers, and communities.

Another valuable aspect of this book is that it is written by a student. The book comes from a student perspective, which is not always heard in the discourse of education reform, this gives the book a unique and honest perspective that is not always present in other books on the subject. It's a powerful reminder that students are often the ones who know best what they need and they must be included in the conversation.

Overall, Achieving Educational Justice: A Narrative of Crusade for Reformation by Apurv Pandey is an inspiring and thought-provoking book that is sure to be a valuable resource for anyone committed to creating a more inclusive and equitable education system. Its unique perspective and call to action make it an essential read for educators, policymakers, and anyone else who wants to understand the complexities of educational justice and the ways in which we can work to achieve it.

It is also worth noting that despite the serious subject matter of the book, Apurv's writing style is engaging and even humorous at times. He infuses his writing with wit and humor, which makes the book not only informative but also enjoyable to read. The book will make you laugh, as well as making you think about the issues of educational justice in a new light.

One example of Apurv's humor is when he writes about how many of the solutions proposed by policymakers and administrators often feel like trying to put a band-aid on a broken leg. He uses this metaphor to illustrate the point that while these solutions may be well-intentioned, they often fail to address the underlying issues and instead only provide a temporary fix.

Another example of Apurv's wit can be seen when he writes about how education is often seen as a "one-size-fits-all" solution to all problems, however, it's not that simple. He points out that just as a "one size fits all" t-shirt never truly fits anyone comfortably, the same goes for education. Each student has unique needs, and it's important to understand that and make an effort to cater to them.

In conclusion, Achieving Educational Justice: A Narrative of Crusade for Reformation by Apurv Pandey is not your typical "dry" educational book. Apurv's writing is engaging and his sense of humor adds an extra layer of enjoyment to the reading experience, while still providing a wealth of information and insights on the subject of educational justice. It's a great read for anyone interested in learning more about the education system and finding ways to make it more fair and just for all students.

Prologue

In "Achieving Educational Justice: A Narrative of Crusade for Reformation," the author takes readers on a journey to uncover the inequalities that exist within our education system and the steps that can be taken to address them. Through personal stories, research, and analysis, the author delves into the systemic issues that perpetuate educational disparities and offers practical solutions for achieving educational justice for all students.

As we continue to grapple with issues of equity and social justice in our society, it is important that we also examine the ways in which these issues manifest in our education system. This book provides a compelling narrative of the challenges faced by marginalized students and their families, and the tireless efforts of educators and advocates working to bring about change.

The author's passion for this subject is evident on every page, and their dedication to achieving educational justice shines through. This book is a powerful call to action for anyone who cares about providing all students with the opportunity to succeed. It should be read and discussed by educators, policymakers, and anyone interested in creating a more just and equitable society.

I highly recommend this book to anyone who wants to learn more about the state of educational justice in our country, and who is committed to working towards a more just and equitable future for all students.

1

Aniket

Aniket was born into a typical family in India, where education was highly valued. From a young age, his parents instilled in him the importance of doing well in school and getting good grades. They believed that this was the key to unlocking a bright future for their son.

However, despite his best efforts, Aniket struggled with his studies. He found it hard to focus in class and had trouble understanding the material being taught. Despite the extra attention and help he received from his teachers and parents, his grades remained poor.

As Aniket grew older, he began to feel like a failure. He saw his classmates excelling in their studies and felt left behind. The pressure to do well in school weighed heavily on him, and he became increasingly disengaged and unmotivated.

As it turns out, Aniket's struggles were not uncommon. The Indian education system, with its heavy emphasis on rote learning and memorization, often fails to address the unique needs and learning styles of its students. Instead of providing a personalized education that helps children to thrive, it pressures them to conform to a one-size-fits-all mold.

Aniket's story is a testament to the many ways in which the Indian education system is failing its students. Its rigid approach to learning stifles creativity and critical thinking, and leaves many children feeling like they don't fit in. Rather than providing children with the tools and support they need to succeed in life, it sets them up for failure.

Aniket's parents had high hopes for their son, but it became a disappointment for them.

The education system should be more inclusive and flexible, and it must focus on meeting the needs of all students, not just those who excel in traditional academic settings. Only then can we hope to provide children like Aniket with the education they need to build successful and fulfilling lives.

As Aniket's struggles with his studies continued, he began to feel isolated and alone. His classmates, who were excelling in their studies, teased and bullied him for his poor grades. They called him names and made fun of him, and Aniket began to feel like an outcast.

The teasing and bullying only made Aniket's struggles worse. He became increasingly disengaged in class, and his grades continued to decline. His teachers, who were overburdened and under-resourced, were unable to provide him with the extra help he needed to catch up. Aniket started to skip classes, feeling like there was no point in going to school. He has lost all the motivation and confidence to attend the school anymore.

At home, his parents were at a loss as to how to help their son. They tried everything they could think of, from hiring private tutors to setting up study schedules, but nothing seemed to work. They felt guilty that they could not provide better education for their son.

Aniket's struggles were not only limited to the school environment, but also extended to the society. His parents and family were shamed in the society for having a son who couldn't make it in school. The shame, the guilt and the disappointment made Aniket's life a living hell. He had no friends and no place where he could fit in.

Despite his struggles with his studies, Aniket's life changed dramatically when he reached class 6. At school, he discovered the game of basketball, and it quickly became his passion. He began to practice every day after school, and soon he was spending all his free time playing and learning more about the sport.

Aniket found that he had a natural talent for basketball, and he started to excel at the game. He joined the school basketball team, and they started winning matches against other schools. His coaches and teammates recognized his talent and encouraged him to continue playing. They saw something special in him and pushed him to be better, which gave Aniket the motivation he needed to continue.

Through basketball, Aniket discovered a new sense of purpose and belonging. He no longer felt like an outcast or a failure in school. He felt like he belonged to a team and had a place in the world. He started to work harder in class, as he needed to maintain his grade level to play. He realized that if he did better in school, he would be able to play for longer.

Basketball also had a positive impact on Aniket's self-esteem. As he became more successful on the court, he began to feel better about himself and his abilities. He started to believe that he could achieve his goals, and that his future was not limited by his poor grades. He could be something, someone.

Aniket's success on the basketball court was recognized by the school, who had never seen him perform so well before. They were happy to see the positive change in him. His parents were proud of him and they were happy that their son had found something he was passionate about and good at. He was soon scouted by a local basketball team, and he started to play in the local tournaments.

As Aniket's love for basketball continued to grow, he began to feel frustrated with the lack of opportunities to play at school. Despite his success on the school team and the positive impact it had on his grades and attitude, the school's focus on academics meant that the basketball team did not have regular practices or matches. Aniket felt like he was being held back from reaching his full potential as a basketball player and it made him more disengaged with school than ever before.

Aniket started to take matters into his own hands, and began to bunk classes to go to the local basketball courts to practice. At first, he felt guilty for not being in school, but as time went on, he became more and more determined to pursue his passion. He was tired of the Indian education system holding him back and wanted to focus on basketball.

It didn't take long for Aniket's absence from school to be noticed by his teachers and parents. His grades started to slip, and he was called in by the school principal for a meeting. The principal tried to convince him to focus on his studies, but Aniket felt like he had nothing to lose. He told him about how he felt being held back by the school's lack of support for basketball and the expectations of society on him.

Aniket's parents were also concerned about his grades and the impact his absenteeism would have on his future. They tried to get him to focus on his studies but he refused to listen. They knew that their son had a passion for basketball, but they were also worried about his education. They didn't want to see their son drop out of school like so many other children they knew who had given up on their dreams.

Aniket's love for basketball had now led him to make a difficult decision, to leave school and focus on basketball. He knew it would be a risk, but he felt that it was his only chance to pursue his dream and make something of himself. Although, he could'nt drop out due to the societal pressures and the road engineers.(According to the author, this term is referred for people who themselves are not successful in life but they give suggestion on **"How to crack IIT by studying NCERT??"**)

ᚦᚦᚦ

2

Bad Means

Aniket's love for basketball led him down a dangerous path as he began to associate with the wrong crowd. As he dropped out of school, he found himself with a lot of free time on his hands, and with no guidance or structure, he started to hang out with the wrong group of people.

One day, Aniket and his new friends were hanging out at the local basketball courts, trying to come up with something to do. One of his friends cracked a joke, "Hey Aniket, you're such a pro at basketball, why not use your skills to hustle a few bucks from the tourists?" And Aniket, who was desperate for money to support himself, thought it was a good idea and they started to organize basketball matches with tourists with high stakes.

> "Slowly, Aniket started to engage in other criminal activities with his friends, as they offered him easy money. He started to steal and sell drugs and he lost sight of what was right and wrong. He had given up on his dream of becoming a basketball player and was now stuck in a cycle of crime and poverty."

Aniket's parents, who had always been supportive of him, were devastated by the changes they saw in their son. They had always known that he had a passion for basketball, but they had never expected it to lead to this. They tried to intervene, but Aniket had become distant and refused to listen to them.

Aniket's story is a tragic reminder of the importance of guidance and support for young people. It is essential for schools, parents, and society to provide children with the resources and support they need to follow their dreams in a healthy and constructive way. It also highlights the dangers of associating with the wrong crowd, and how easy it is to fall into the wrong path when one is not provided with the necessary support.

It's important to remember, following your passion is great, but not at the cost of losing oneself and committing wrong actions. One should always try to find a balance and make sure that the road taken is the right one.

As Aniket reached his teenage years, he began to realize that the life he had chosen for himself was not as fulfilling as he had hoped. He had given up on his dream of becoming a professional basketball player and was instead using malpractices to make money. He started to feel empty and lost as he went through the motions of committing crimes day by day.

One day, Aniket was caught by the police for his involvement in a theft case. As he sat in the cell, he had a lot of time to think about the choices he had made. He remembered the advice that his mother used to give him when he was younger, "If you want to go fast, go alone, if you want to go far, go together." He realized that he had chosen the fast route, but it had led him nowhere.

Aniket's time in jail also made him realize that the true meaning of life was not just for those who studied. It was for those who had a purpose, a passion and worked hard towards it. He realized that he had let his passion slip away and had chosen the easy route to make money, without considering the consequences.

He also met few people in the jail who had made the same mistakes as he had and were repenting for the same. They had given up on their dreams and had landed themselves in the same situation as him. Aniket realized that the life he had chosen for himself was not the one he wanted and he decided to make a change.

Upon his release, Aniket decided to go back to school and get his education. He realized that education was not just about getting good marks and pleasing society, but also about gaining knowledge and skills that would help him in life. He also took up basketball again, but this time as a way to stay out of trouble and stay focused on his studies.

Aniket's story is a reminder that it's never too late to change course and make a fresh start. As the old saying goes, "It's never too late to mend." With hard work and determination, Aniket was able to turn his life around and build a better future for himself. It also highlights the importance of purpose and passion in one's life, and the dangers of taking the easy route.

Having a hard time focusing on studies and basketball as well

As Aniket returned to school, he found that he had to balance his studies and his passion for basketball. It was not an easy task, and he often found himself struggling to keep up with both. But he was determined to make it work and was committed to his goals.

However, as he entered his teenage years, Aniket found himself getting attracted to girls. He started to spend a lot of time thinking about them and getting distracted from his studies and basketball practice. He would often daydream about them during class and would lose focus on his studies.

This made it difficult for him to keep up with his studies and he started to fall behind. He also found that he was not able to perform as well on the basketball court as he was not giving it his full attention. He was in a dilemma, not able to focus on either of his passion.

He knew that something had to give and he had to make a choice, either to focus on his studies or on girls. It was a tough decision, but he knew that he couldn't let his attraction to girls interfere with his goals and his future.

Aniket decided to put a little distance between himself and the girl he was interested in, and focus on his studies and basketball. It was not easy, but he knew it was the right thing to do.

As time passed, Aniket was able to regain his focus and was able to catch up with his studies. He also saw improvement in his basketball performance, as he was able to give it his full attention. He also realized that love and attraction can wait, but opportunities for education and passion might not.

Aniket's story is a reminder that, as a teenager, it's natural to have different interests and attractions, but it's important to be able to balance and prioritize them so that they don't interfere with our goals and dreams. As the old saying goes, "All work and no play makes Jack a dull boy." It's important to find a balance and not let one aspect of life completely consume us.

As Aniket settled back into school, he found that making friends was not as easy as it used to be. He was older now and many of his classmates had already formed tight-knit groups, leaving him feeling like an outsider.

One day, while passing through the school playground, Aniket noticed a new student playing basketball alone. The new student, Eric, was not very good, but Aniket could tell that he had a passion for the game. Aniket decided to introduce himself and offer to play a game with Eric.

"Hey, I couldn't help but notice your form needs some work, want me to give you some pointers?" Aniket asked, trying to lighten the mood with a joke.

Eric laughed and thanked Aniket for the offer. From that day forward, Aniket and Eric became inseparable friends. They had a lot in common, as Eric was also struggling in school and had a passion for basketball. They would spend hours practicing together and discussing their dreams of becoming professional basketball players.

Aniket and Eric's friendship was a beacon of hope for Aniket, who had been feeling lost and alone. They were able to understand each other's struggles and support each other through the difficult times.

As they spent more time together, they started to realize that they needed to set some boundaries. They found that they were spending too much time on leisure activities, watching movies and playing video games, neglecting their studies. They realized that they were wasting their time and it was causing them to fall behind in school. They knew that they needed to find a balance and focus on their studies, in addition to their passion for basketball.

As the old saying goes, "Time and tide wait for no man." Aniket and Eric knew that they couldn't afford to waste any more time. They set themselves a strict schedule, making sure to prioritize their studies, basketball practice and leisure time in a balanced way. With hard work and determination, Aniket and Eric were able to catch up with their studies and improve their basketball skills.

Aniket's story highlights the importance of friendship and support in achieving our goals. It also emphasizes that it's crucial to find a balance in life and not let one aspect consume us

As Aniket and Eric continued to work towards their goals, Aniket found himself struggling with his studies. Despite putting in the time and effort, he was unable to make progress and his grades were not improving. This left him feeling frustrated and demotivated.

One day, Aniket confided in Eric about his struggles. "I just don't get it, Eric," Aniket exclaimed, "I sit down to study every day, but the material just doesn't seem to stick. I feel like I'm stuck in a rut."

Eric, being a good friend, offered his support. "Listen, Aniket, I know how you feel. I've been there myself. But, you can't let it get to you. Just remember, 'Rome wasn't built in a day.' You're not going to master a subject overnight."

Aniket took Eric's words to heart and decided to take a different approach. He realized that he needed to take a step back and reflect on his study habits. He began to introspect himself, analysing where he was going wrong and what he could do to improve.

He started to talk to his teachers and seek help. He realized that his problem was not with his intelligence but with the way he studied. He lacked effective studying methods and strategies. His teachers helped him to adopt a more efficient way of studying and helped him to improve his study habits.

Aniket also started to change his attitude towards studies, instead of seeing it as a chore, he started to see it as a challenge and an opportunity to learn something new. He started to enjoy learning and found that it was no longer as difficult as before.

As his grades began to improve, Aniket couldn't help but to let out a chuckle and say, "Eric, I think we need to change that old saying, 'Rome wasn't built.

As Aniket's grades improved, he and Eric started to spend more time discussing the struggles they had faced and the lessons they had learned. They would often talk about the harsh realities of the world and how the education system often seemed designed to hold people back, rather than help them succeed.

One day, as they were walking to class, Eric turned to Aniket and said, "You know, it's a cruel world out there. It's like the old saying 'Life is a grindstone. Whether it grinds us down or polishes us up depends on us.'"

Aniket nodded in agreement, "It's true, the education system often seems to be more concerned with churning out good test takers, rather than fostering creative and independent thinkers."

"Exactly," Eric said, "It's like they want to make us all into little robots, all the same and compliant. But you and I know that true success comes from thinking outside the box, and not just regurgitating what we're taught."

Aniket laughed, "You know, I never thought of it like that before. But you're right, we need to be more like the 'black sheep' and less like the 'sheep in a flock'"

The two friends continued to have conversations like these, discussing the challenges they faced and the lessons they had learned. They supported each other and helped each other to navigate the often harsh and unforgiving world.

Their friendship was a reminder that even in the darkest of times, there is always hope. And that, as the old saying goes "A friend in need is a friend indeed." Together, they were able to overcome the obstacles that the education system and the world had put in their way, and build a brighter future for themselves.

As Aniket and Eric continued to work towards their goals, they started to have more profound conversations about the world and the difficulties they would face. Aniket, who had been through a lot, had a more jaded view of the world and the challenges they would face.

"Eric," Aniket said, "I fear that the world is a cruel and unforgiving place. The road to success is fraught with obstacles and pitfalls. How do you think we can overcome these challenges?"

Eric, being the optimist, replied, "Aniket, I understand your concerns. But, I believe that the world is what we make of it. Sure, there will be obstacles, but we must persevere and not let them defeat us. We mustn't be daunted by the vicissitudes of fortune and always look for opportunities amidst difficulties."

Aniket was impressed by Eric's words and began to see things from a different perspective. He realized that Eric was right, that the world was not inherently cruel but it was how he perceived it. He began to see opportunities where he once saw obstacles.

They both realized that to succeed in life, they must be adaptable and resilient. They knew that they would face challenges and setbacks, but they also knew that they had the strength to overcome them. As Eric put it, "A smooth sea never made a skillful sailor" They both knew that they would have to navigate through rough waters to reach their destination.

Aniket and Eric's conversation highlighted the importance of having a positive mindset and a "can-do" attitude in life. It emphasized that with determination and perseverance, one can overcome any obstacles that life may throw their way.

As Aniket and Eric's friendship grew, they continued to work towards their goals, supporting each other through the ups and downs. They faced many challenges together, but they always found a way to overcome them.

Aniket's grades continued to improve and he was able to achieve the grades he needed to enroll in college. Eric, who had been struggling to make the basketball team, was able to improve his skills with the help of Aniket and was eventually able to make the team.

They both decided to pursue their passion for basketball and went to college on scholarships. They were able to make a name for themselves as talented basketball players, and Aniket's dream of becoming a professional basketball player was finally within reach.

Their friendship was also a testament of the importance of having people in your life who truly understand you and support you. Aniket and Eric were able to achieve their dreams because they were able to rely on each other's support and encouragement. As Eric said, "Friends are the family we choose."

Aniket and Eric's story is one of determination, perseverance, and the power of friendship. It shows that with hard work and the right attitude, one can overcome any obstacle and achieve their dreams. It also illustrates how important it is to have someone who truly understands you and supports you in your journey through life.

ᑭᑭᑭ

3

The Turning Point

As Aniket entered his teenage years, he faced a new set of challenges, both in his studies and in his personal life. One day, while he was in class, a teacher embarrassed him in front of his classmates. The teacher had scolded Aniket for not paying attention in class and had singled him out in front of the whole class.

Aniket, feeling humiliated and angry, left the classroom and didn't come back for the rest of the day. He felt like he was not understood by anyone, not even his teacher. This experience left a deep impact on him, and he started to have a negative attitude towards studies and school.

He started to feel like a misfit in the school and started to act out, disobeying school rules and getting into fights. He was constantly angry and had a chip on his shoulder.

Eric, who was Aniket's best friend, tried to intervene, but Aniket would not listen to him. Eric said, "Aniket, 'You can't make a silk purse out of a sow's ear' don't let one bad experience define who you are." But Aniket was too angry and bitter to listen to reason.

As time passed, Aniket's behavior only worsened the school administration and parents, but it made him more isolated, as he lost his friends, his teachers trust and respect. He stopped caring about his studies and stopped going to school regularly. He felt like he had nothing left to lose.

Aniket's story highlights the importance of understanding and empathy when dealing with troubled teens, especially when they are facing difficult situations like the one Aniket had experienced.

As Aniket's negative attitude towards school and studies persisted, he began to look for outlets to escape his problems. He started experimenting with smoking and drinking, frequently sneaking out to bars at the age of 15.

He soon found himself hanging out with a group of older teens, who were also involved in a life of smoking, drinking and partying. They were not good influences, they were involved in various illegal activities.

Aniket quickly became entrenched in this new lifestyle, and his behavior became increasingly erratic. He would come home late, drunk and high, and would often get into fights with his parents. He was breaking many laws for his age, like buying cigarettes, alcohol and even getting into bars, where he didn't have the legal age.

His school grades started to suffer and he got into a lot of trouble with the law enforcement. He was always on the edge of getting arrested, but he was too young for it. He was not only breaking the laws but also his future.

Eric, who had stuck by Aniket throughout his troubles, was deeply concerned about his friend's descent into a life of substance abuse and criminal activity. He tried to intervene and help Aniket, but his efforts were in vain. Aniket had become too entrenched in his new lifestyle and refused to listen to reason.

Aniket's story highlights the dangers of substance abuse and the negative impact it can have on one's life, especially when combined with a lack of guidance and positive influences. It also demonstrates how easy it is for young people to get sucked into a life of crime and how difficult it can be to turn back. It is crucial for society to have appropriate support and educational systems for the youth, so they don't have to resort to such drastic measures.

As Aniket's downward spiral continued, he became increasingly disenchanted with the world around him. He felt like no one understood him and that he didn't fit in. In search of solace, he turned to the literature of Charles Bukowski, a controversial author known for his dark, unapologetic portrayals of the seedy underbelly of society.

Aniket was drawn to Bukowski's raw, unvarnished writing style and the way he depicted the gritty reality of the world reading the book titling "The Subtle Art of not giving a F__k". He saw himself in Bukowski's characters and found comfort in their struggles. He would spend hours reading Bukowski's work, devouring everything he could find.

"Well, if Bukowski can survive in this world, I guess I can too," Aniket would often quip, trying to find humor in the bleakness of his situation.

But Aniket's immersion in Bukowski's world soon led him to adopt some of the author's more self-destructive habits. He began to drink heavily and to engage in reckless behavior, all in an attempt to emulate his literary hero.

Eric, who had been worried about Aniket's well-being, watched in dismay as his friend continued to spiral out of control. "Aniket, you can't change who you are to fit into someone else's idea of cool or success. 'Be yourself, everyone else is already taken.' Bukowski's lifestyle may have worked for him, but it's not the only way to live," Eric tried to reason with him.

But Aniket refused to listen, too lost in his admiration for Bukowski. He continued to follow the author's example, ultimately leading to more trouble and negative consequences in his life.

Aniket's story illustrates the dangers of hero worship and the need for individuals to find their own unique path in life. It also shows how the art and literature we consume can impact our worldview and the choices we make. It is important to find role models and inspiration, but not to become lost in them and lose oneself in the process.

As Aniket's reckless behavior continued, he found himself increasingly unhappy. Despite the initial thrill of living on the edge, he soon realized that his constant search for excitement and escape was not bringing him the fulfillment he sought.

"Why is it that the more I try to escape my problems, the more they seem to follow me?" Aniket said to Eric in a moment of introspection, "I suppose it's true what they say, 'You can't run away from your problems, they will always catch up to you.'"

Aniket began to see that his constant pursuit of pleasure and distraction was not leading him to happiness, but only to more problems. He felt trapped in a cycle of self-destruction, unable to break free from his destructive habits.

As he reflected on his life, Aniket realized that happiness was not something that could be chased or attained through external means. He understood that true happiness comes from within, and that it was up to him to find it.

Aniket began to make small changes in his life, trying to find things that truly made him happy. He started to spend more time with Eric and his family, took up a hobby, and even started to attend school again. He started to take responsibility for his own happiness, instead of looking to others or external factors to bring him joy.

Through these small actions, Aniket slowly started to regain a sense of purpose and direction in his life. He came to realize that true happiness is not about chasing pleasure, but about finding meaning and fulfillment in one's life. He learned that "the greatest wealth is to live content with little," a proverb that he always kept in mind.

Aniket's story highlights the importance of finding inner happiness and the dangers of chasing external pleasures as a means to find fulfillment. It also shows that true happiness is not a destination, but a journey, and that it requires effort and self-reflection to find and maintain.

This introspection by Aniket was not by self but from a external sources. Let's know that in the next few chapters.

ᐳᐳᐳ

4

The Beam of Light

As Aniket began to navigate his new approach to life, he found himself struggling to find a sense of direction and purpose. But, just when things seemed to be at their bleakest, he met a new teacher named Sahil Sir.

Sahil was unlike any teacher Aniket had ever met. He had a unique teaching style and approach that struck a chord with Aniket. Sahil was able to connect with his students on a personal level, and he had a profound impact on Aniket's life.

Aniket found himself going to Sahil's class every day, eager to learn more. Sahil saw Aniket's potential and encouraged him to pursue his goals and interests. He pushed him to think critically, to ask questions, and to be curious about the world around him.

Aniket would often joke with Sahil, "Looks like you're the 'light at the end of the tunnel' that I've been searching for."

One day, after class, Aniket approached Sahil and struck up a conversation. "Sir, I don't know how to express my gratitude for what you've done for me. I feel like a completely different person since I started attending your class."

Sahil smiled and replied, "Aniket, I'm glad to hear that. Remember, 'Give a man a fish and you feed him for a day. Teach a man to fish and you feed him for a lifetime.' I didn't change you, I simply gave you the tools to change yourself."

Aniket realized that Sahil was right, he had given him the guidance and support he needed to find his own path in life. Aniket began to work harder in school, and he started to see a future for himself. He realized that his potential was limitless, and that with the right mindset, anything was possible.

Aniket's story illustrates the powerful impact that a good teacher can have on a student's life. It shows how a teacher can inspire and guide students, providing them with the tools and confidence they need to succeed.

As Aniket continued to work towards a better life, he decided to explore new methods to improve his mental and physical well-being. He started to practice yoga and meditation to bring some balance and peace in his life. He also made a conscious effort to do good deeds, to help others and to give back to the community.

Aniket soon found that these practices had a transformative effect on his life. He felt more grounded and focused, and his relationships with others also improved. He started to become more empathetic, compassionate and had a better understanding of the people and the world around him.

One day, Aniket's friend Eric asked him, "Aniket, what's the deal with all this yoga and good deeds? You're like a totally different person now. "

Aniket replied with a chuckle, "Well Eric, they say 'A healthy body, a healthy mind', and I've realized that in order to be truly happy, I need to take care of both. Plus, 'Charity begins at home' and I figured why not start with myself first."

Eric was intrigued by Aniket's newfound perspective, and he decided to give yoga and meditation a try for himself. He was amazed by the positive changes he saw in himself, and he started to adopt a more positive and compassionate outlook on life.

Aniket's friends and family also noticed a change in him. He was happier, more content, and he seemed to have a better understanding of himself and the world around him. He was also more dedicated to his studies and work, he was more focused and made more conscious choices.

As Aniket continued to explore yoga and meditation, he also started to incorporate it in his conversations with his friends. He would often use yoga and meditation as a metaphor in his conversations, using it as a way to express his thoughts and ideas in a more poetic and nuanced way.

For example, when discussing a difficult problem with Eric, Aniket would say "It's like trying to hold a warrior pose, it's uncomfortable and challenging, but if we hold on, we'll eventually find balance and inner strength."

Eric would often be surprised by the depth and meaning behind Aniket's words and he would have to ask for clarification.

Aniket would then explain the double-meaning behind his words. "It's like when we're in warrior pose, we're faced with a difficult task and it may seem uncomfortable but we need to push through and find balance. In this situation, the problem we're facing is the warrior pose, if we push through and stay focused, we'll find a solution and come out stronger."

Aniket's friends also started to adopt this style of speaking and it became a common joke among them. They would often tease each other by talking in yoga metaphors and it was a way for them to bond and express themselves in a more creative way.

Aniket's journey illustrates the powerful ways that yoga and meditation can bring balance, inner peace, and a deeper understanding of oneself and the world. His unique approach to communication also highlights the potential for using poetry and metaphor to express oneself in a more nuanced and meaningful way. It also shows how incorporating such practices into daily life.

As Aniket's understanding of the world and himself deepened, he also found a new appreciation for dark humor and jokes. He would often use dark humor to express his thoughts and ideas in a way that was both humorous and thought-provoking.

For example, when discussing the state of the world with Eric, Aniket would say "The world is like a rollercoaster, it's full of ups and downs, but at least it's not a merry-go-round, that thing's just going in circles."

Eric, who was also a fan of dark humor, would understand the underlying message in Aniket's joke and respond with a wry grin, "Yup, the world may be a mess but at least it's not boring."

In another conversation, Aniket would say "Sometimes, it feels like life is just one big game of Russian roulette, you never know when your time's up."

This type of conversation was a way for them to express their thoughts and feelings about difficult and heavy topics in a more lighthearted and humorous way. It allowed them to process and understand complex and difficult issues in a more digestible and manageable way.

It's important to note that dark humor is not for everyone and can be offensive and distasteful to some people. it should be used carefully and with the knowledge of the audience. Not everyone will understand or appreciate a dark joke, it is important to be mindful of how your words might be received.

Aniket's journey of self-discovery and personal growth began when he started to practice yoga and meditation. These practices helped him to become more mindful and present in the moment. He learned to quiet his mind and focus on his breath, which in turn helped him to become more aware of his thoughts, emotions, and actions.

Through the practice of yoga and meditation, Aniket began to understand the concept of introspection. He learned to observe his thoughts and feelings without judgment, and to understand their underlying causes. He became more aware of how his thoughts and actions affected his mood, relationships and overall well-being. He also realized that his thoughts and emotions were not facts, but rather fleeting and changing experiences that could be observed, understood and eventually released.

Aniket also began to read books and articles about self-reflection, self-awareness and introspection. He learned about different techniques such as journaling, self-inquiry, and inner dialogue. He would often spend time meditating, journaling and reflecting on the events of the day, noting down his thoughts and emotions and understanding the patterns and root cause of those thoughts.

Through his exploration, Aniket learned to be more compassionate towards himself, and to understand that change and growth take time. He learned that introspection is not a one-time event, but a continuous process of becoming more self-aware and understanding oneself better. He also understood that introspection allows one to have a better understanding of one's own behavior and emotions, which ultimately leads to better decision-making, better relationships and overall well-being.

As Aniket continued to grow and develop, he also started to explore new interests and hobbies. One of the things he became interested in was poetry, specifically the works of William Wordsworth. He found that the poet's words spoke to him on a deep and personal level, and he would often spend hours reading and studying his works.

One day, while reading Wordsworth's poetry in a local park, Aniket struck up a conversation with a stranger who was also reading a book of poetry. As they talked, they discovered that they both shared a love of Wordsworth's works and had a deep appreciation for the beauty of nature.

They introduced themselves, and the stranger's name was Sophia. They became friends quickly, they would often meet in the park and read Wordsworth's poetry together, discussing the meanings and interpretations of the poet's words. They would also take walks in nature and appreciate the beauty of the world around them, something that Wordsworth often wrote about.

Sophia became a great friend of Aniket's, and their shared love for poetry and nature brought them closer together. They would often talk about their understanding of the world and how poetry can bring solace and inspiration in difficult times.

Aniket's friendship with Sophia is an excellent example of how shared interests can bring people together and form deep and meaningful connections. It also shows how poetry and literature can serve as a bridge for people to connect and understand each other in a unique way. It also highlights how appreciation of art and beauty, particularly in nature, can serve as a common ground for connection and friendship.

Sophia and Aniket's friendship was not only built on their shared love for Wordsworth's poetry, but also their sense of humor. They would often use Wordsworth's poetry as inspiration for their own jokes and puns. They would make each other laugh by twisting the poet's words in unexpected ways, and it became a playful game for them to enjoy.

For example, while reading "I Wandered Lonely as a Cloud" Aniket would say "I wandered lonely as a cloud, that floats on high o'er vales and hills, unless of course, I'm in the city, then I'm just a cloud that floats on high o'er traffic and pollution"

Sophia would laugh and reply with her own joke "When I have fears that I may cease to be, before my pen has glean'd my teeming brain, unless of course, I'm at a party, then I have fears that I may cease to be, before my drink is finished"

Their jokes and puns on Wordsworth poems not only added an element of playfulness to their friendship but it also helped them to understand the poetry better, by taking the words less seriously and looking at the poetry from different perspective. It also showed how literature and poetry can be enjoyed in multiple ways, and doesn't always have to be read with a serious tone.

Through these jokes and puns, Sophia and Aniket were able to deepen their understanding of Wordsworth's poetry and develop a deeper appreciation for the beauty of language and wordplay. It also serves as a reminder that literature and poetry can be enjoyed in different ways and it's not always necessary to be serious and stuffy when approaching it.

As Sophia and Aniket spent more time together, their conversations became more profound, and they began to explore deeper and more meaningful topics. One of the subjects that came up frequently in their discussions was the concept of God and the creation of the universe.

Aniket, who had been raised in a religious household, had always had a strong belief in God and the afterlife. Sophia, on the other hand, had a more scientific worldview and questioned the existence of God and the idea of creation.

Aniket and Sophia would often have lively debates and discussions about the topic, and they were able to learn and understand each other's perspectives. They talked about the different ways in which people perceive the world, and the role of faith and reason in shaping one's beliefs.

Sophia would often ask Aniket, "If God created everything, who created God?" Aniket would respond "God is the uncaused cause, the beginning and the end, the alpha and the omega"

Sophia would also inquire "How do you explain the intricacies and beauty of the natural world without the concept of a creator?" Aniket would reply "The beauty of nature is evidence of the creator's existence, it's like looking at a painting, one can see the brushstrokes of the artist."

Despite their differing views, Sophia and Aniket were able to have civil and respectful conversations. They learned to appreciate each other's perspectives and the complexity of the subject. Through their conversations, they learned to respect each other's beliefs, and they realized that the quest for understanding is never-ending and that one's beliefs may change over time.

These conversations also highlighted the importance of open-mindedness and being able to consider different perspectives when discussing deep and meaningful topics. It shows how two people with different views can still come together and have a respectful and meaningful dialogue.

Through their shared love of poetry and nature, as well as their deep and meaningful conversations about God and creation, Sophia and Aniket developed a deep and enduring friendship.

They would often spend their weekends together, going on hikes in the mountains, reading poetry by the river, or simply sitting in the park, talking and laughing. They would support each other through the challenges and struggles they faced, both in their personal and professional lives.

As they got to know each other better, they found that they had many things in common, such as a love of books, a sense of adventure and a desire to make the world a better place. They would often have long conversations about their hopes and dreams, and they would encourage each other to pursue their passions and aspirations.

Aniket found in Sophia a confidant, someone who could understand and accept him for who he was, and with whom he could share his thoughts and feelings without fear of judgment. Sophia, in turn, found in Aniket a loyal and supportive friend, someone who was always there for her and who helped her to see the world in a new and more positive light.

As their friendship grew, Aniket and Sophia found that they had become best friends, their bond was unbreakable, their trust and understanding grew day by day. Their friendship was the shining light in each of their lives, and they knew that it was a friendship that would last a lifetime.

Their friendship serves as an example of how shared interests, open-mindedness, and deep conversations can bring people together and lead to strong and lasting bonds. It highlights the importance of having supportive and understanding friends in one's life and how it can change one's perspective, bring meaning and happiness.

ppp

5

Passion for Poems

Aniket's friendship with Sophia was a major factor in his passion for poetry. Sophia, who had been a lover of poetry for many years, introduced him to the works of William Wordsworth and other poets, and it was through these works that Aniket discovered his own love of poetry.

Sophia would often take him to poetry readings and workshops, where he would be exposed to new and diverse poets, which helped him to explore different styles and forms of poetry. She would also share her own insights and interpretations of the poems, which helped Aniket to develop a deeper understanding and appreciation for the works.

Under Sophia's guidance and encouragement, Aniket began to explore poetry as a form of self-expression. He started to write his own poems, using it as a way to express his feelings, thoughts and emotions. Sophia would often give him feedback, help him in correcting his poems and encouraging him to continue.

With Sophia's support and guidance, Aniket's love and passion for poetry deepened. He found that poetry was not just a form of artistic expression, but also a way to connect with others, make sense of the world, and express his understanding of the world. He realized that poetry was a way to look at the world differently, and it was this passion that helped Aniket to develop a more profound and nuanced view of the world.

Aniket's journey into poetry illustrates how the influence of someone we admire and look up to can shape our interests and passions. It shows how the guidance and support of a friend can help us to explore and develop new interests, and how it can lead to personal growth and self-discovery.

Here are some stock poems written by Aniket during love for poems:

ᐅᐅᐅ

Aniket's Life

"Aniket's life, a journey of growth and change,

A path filled with ups and downs, twists and turns.

He started as a boy in a middle-class home,

With dreams of greatness, but feeling alone.

He struggled with studies, felt out of place,

His grades not reflecting his efforts and grace.

But basketball became his saving grace,

A passion that would put him in first place.

He bunked classes, and made friends not so true,

As he searched for acceptance, and something to do.

But his teenage years brought a different view,

He fell into bad habits, and all that was new.

Until he met Eric, a friend who was true,

Together they laughed, and felt the blues.

As they talked and grew, Aniket came to see,

That happiness is a problem, and introspection the key.

Through yoga and good deeds, he learned to be still,

To look within himself, and see what he will.

But it was Sophia, a friend in a unique way,

Through poetry, they shared a bond, each and every day.

Aniket's life, a journey with many a tale,

But through it all, he learned to stand tall and prevail."

Failing Education System: A Elegy of Dysfunction

"*I wandered lonely as a cloud*

Through classrooms dark and dull

Where knowledge scarce, and learning flawed

The students' minds did pull.

The teacher's voice did echo on

Through halls of disarray

Where textbooks old, and standards low

Did blight the pupils' day.

And oft I heard the students say

"We're lost in this abyss

Our futures dim, our spirits grim

Because of this failing bliss."

But nature's beauty still remains

In fields and hills and streams

And so, I hope that one day soon

Education too, will gleam.

But for now, alas, the clouds do hang

Low in the sky so gray

A symbol of the education system

That leads us all astray."

Failing Democracy: A Lament of Perverted Sovereignty Democracy: When Freedom Goes Insane

"Amidst the clamor of the crowd,

Amidst the strife of tongues,

A nation's hope for liberty

Is strangled by the lungs

Of those who would subvert the will

Of the people they are meant to serve

And warp the very principles

Upon which democracy doth nerve.

The hallowed halls of governance

Are fraught with venal strife

Where greed and power are the siren's song

That leads our leaders to the brink of life.

And thus, the dream of independence

That once did our forefathers inspire

Is now but a forlorn illusion

That doth our spirits tire

With each passing day, the beacon of freedom

Dims in the sky above

As the hands of the corrupted few

Clutch tighter the reins of power and love

And the people, caught in the web of lies

Are left to languish in despair

While the shadow of despotism creeps

Ever closer, unaware.

This is the bitter fruit of failing democracy

This is the price of independence betrayed

And until we reclaim our sovereignty

And the rights for which our forefathers prayed

We shall forever be shackled

To the chains of a republic degraded."

Empyrean Bond: A Ode to Friendship

Friendship is a treasure rare,

A bond that knows no bound,

A shining light that guides us through

Life's darkest, roughest round.

It is a bridge that spans the chasms

Of life's changing sea,

A steadfast companion through the storms

That rage and howl and flee.

It is a hand that lends support

In times of need and woe,

A listening ear that hears the heart

And helps it's secrets flow.

It is a mirror that reflects

The beauty in the soul,

A celebration of the self

And the love that makes us whole.

With each step we take together

The bond grows strong and true,

For with a friend beside us

We can conquer all we do.

Friendship is a precious gem

That glows with inner fire,

It's radiance shines throughout our lives

With warmth that can inspire."

Beacons of Friendship: An Ode to Eric and Sophia

"*Eric and Sophia, friends so true,*

Guiding lights that shone anew,

Through life's journey, dark and long,

They helped Aniket find his song.

With laughter shared and tales to tell,

They walked the path with him through hell,

And when the road seemed rough and steep,

Eric and Sophia helped him keep.

With steady hand and guiding light,

They showed him wrong from wrong and right,

And when the doubts and fears crept in,

They helped him find the strength within.

Through joy and pain, through love and loss,

Their friendship proved to be the boss,

A bond unbreakable, a love so pure,

With Eric and Sophia, Aniket felt secure.

And now as they part ways,

and journey on their own,

Aniket will always cherish,

the memories they've shown.

For Eric and Sophia,

will always be in his heart

guiding him, even though they are apart."

6
Aniket's J-curve

With the guidance of Sahil sir, Eric, and Sophia, Aniket's life took a new direction. He put in extra effort to improve his academics and, with hard work and dedication, he was able to achieve good grades. He also excelled in basketball, becoming a star player on his school team.

Sahil Sir recognized his potential and helped him to gain a scholarship for a university with strong sports and academics programs. Aniket was able to pursue higher education and continue playing basketball at a competitive level.

Aniket's success in both academics and sports eventually led to him being recruited to play professional basketball for the state. He never forgot the lessons and values that Eric, Sophia and Sahil Sir had taught him and always made sure to give back to his community.

The story of Aniket, Eric, Sophia and Sahil Sir is one of determination, friendship and the power of guidance and mentorship. They all helped each other to reach their full potential and become the best versions of themselves, showing that with hard work, dedication and a support system, one can overcome any obstacle and achieve great things in life.

As Aniket progressed to class 9, his dedication to both academics and basketball paid off. He secured excellent marks and the pride of his parents knew no bounds. They were overjoyed to see their son excel in a way they never thought possible. They often joked about how they would have never believed that their son, who once struggled with academics, would one day make them so proud.

Aniket was thrilled to see the joy on his parents' faces and knew that it was all thanks to the guidance of Sahil Sir, the encouragement of Eric and Sophia, and his own perseverance. As he basked in the glory of his achievements, he couldn't help but reflect on how far he had come.

One evening, Aniket was sitting in the living room with his parents, discussing his future plans, when his father jokingly said, "Son, you've made us so proud. I never thought I'd see the day when you'd become a scholar-athlete." Aniket laughed along, but inside he felt a twinge of humility. He knew that his parents' unwavering support had been a key factor in his success.

"I couldn't have done it without you guys," Aniket said, his voice filled with gratitude. "And of course, without the guidance of Sahil Sir, and the friendship of Eric and Sophia."

His mother smiled and nodded. "We're so glad you had such wonderful people in your life to help guide you. They really made a difference."

Aniket agreed wholeheartedly. "They truly did. And I will always be grateful to them."

As they continued to talk and reminisce about Aniket's journey, they all laughed and shared some jokes and conversations together, feeling happy and content. They knew that this was just the beginning, and that there would be many more achievements and successes to come.

Aniket knew that the road ahead would not be easy, but with the support of his family, the guidance of Sahil Sir, the encouragement of Eric and Sophia, and his own perseverance, he was confident that he could achieve anything he set his mind to.

As Aniket continued to excel in both academics and basketball, he began to take a keen interest in the education system. He noticed that despite his own success, many of his classmates were still struggling to keep up. He was particularly troubled by the rigid and outdated teaching methods that seemed to stifle creativity and critical thinking.

He began to speak out against the system, using his wit and humor to get his message across. He would often make jokes and use proverbs to drive home the point that the education system needed to change. He would often say things like "You can't make a silk purse out of a sow's ear" to emphasize that the current system was not capable of producing successful students.

His classmates found his jokes and proverbs both amusing and enlightening. They began to look at the education system in a new light and started to demand change. Aniket's wit and humor had sparked a revolution and it wasn't long before the school administration was forced to take notice.

His teacher Sahil Sir, who had been a mentor and guide throughout his school days, recognized the importance of Aniket's ideas and started to implement them in his classroom. He began to incorporate more interactive and student-centered teaching methods, which helped to engage the students and made learning more fun and interactive.

Aniket's impact on the education system was palpable, and it wasn't long before other schools in the area started to take notice. With his clever wit, Aniket had managed to spark a change that would benefit countless students for years to come.

As Aniket graduated from high school and moved on to college, he was proud to see that the change he had started was continuing to grow and evolve. He knew that he had made a difference and that his jokes and proverbs had played a key role in helping to make the education system better for future generations.

As Aniket continued to excel in both academics and sports, his popularity and reputation began to grow. He was invited to join various clubs and societies, and he quickly found himself in the center of a large and diverse group of friends.

Aniket, basking in the adulation of his newfound circle, began to develop a sense of self-importance. He thought of himself as something great, a shining star in a sea of mediocrity. He surrounded himself with people who would sing his praises and eagerly accepted their flattery, he was living in a comfort zone.

His old friends, Eric and Sophia, noticed the change in Aniket and were concerned about the shift in his attitude. They recognized that his newfound sense of self-importance was causing him to become increasingly isolated from the people who truly cared about him.

One evening, Eric and Sophia decided to intervene. They invited Aniket to a gathering of their old friends, who included a group of talented rappers. They had planned a surprise for Aniket, and as he arrived, they launched into a rap that they had composed especially for him.

The rap was a cleverly-worded critique of Aniket's new attitude. It highlighted the importance of humility and gratitude and how those traits are what truly make a person great. It also reminded Aniket that true friends will always be there to tell the truth, even if it's hard to hear.

The rap caught Aniket off guard, but it made him realize that he had been living in a bubble of self-importance. He felt humbled by his friends' words and ashamed of how he had been behaving. He apologized to Eric and Sophia, and to his old friends, for his attitude and thanked them for their honesty.

With the help of his closest friends, Aniket was able to see the error of his ways and recommitted himself to humility and gratitude. He realized that true greatness is not measured by fame or wealth, but by the way we treat others and by how much we are willing to give back to the community.

Aniket recognized that being surrounded by friends who were not afraid to tell the truth, even when it was uncomfortable, was more valuable than any amount of flattery and praise. He learned that it's more important to stay true to oneself rather than to chase after fame and recognition, he decided to never be trapped in his own comfort zone again.

As Aniket became more and more successful, he found himself spending more and more time on social media. He loved the attention and validation he received from his peers and the public. He would often post about his achievements, both academic and athletic, as well as photos of himself with his friends and family. He also enjoyed reading and responding to the messages and comments from his followers.

Initially, Aniket enjoyed the positive feedback and attention he received on social media, but as time went on, he began to become addicted to it. He would check his phone constantly throughout the day, compulsively scrolling through his feed, seeking validation and approval. He became increasingly focused on getting more likes, comments, and followers, to the point that it began to interfere with his daily life.

His friends and family noticed the change in him, and they were concerned. They could see that he was spending more and more time on his phone and that he was becoming more and more obsessed with his social media presence. They tried to talk to him about it, but he was in denial. He thought that his addiction to social media was helping him to stay connected with his friends and followers, and that it was a normal part of life.

Aniket's obsession with social media eventually began to affect his relationships, his school work and his overall well-being. He would often stay up late responding to comments and messages, and would even neglect his homework and studies because of it. He would also miss out on opportunities to spend time with his friends and family because he was too busy on social media.

Realizing the gravity of the situation, Aniket sought help. He met with a therapist who helped him to understand the impact that social media addiction can have on an individual's life. Aniket slowly but surely started to regain control over his life. He set limits on his social media usage, deleted some apps and unfollowed some accounts that were triggering him to spend too much time on it. He also started to spend more time engaging in activities that he enjoyed such as playing basketball, reading and spending time with his loved ones.

Aniket learned the hard way, how easy it is to fall into the trap of social media addiction and how detrimental it can be to one's well-being. He now knows that it's important to set limits, to be aware of one's actions and to not let it consume one's life.

Aniket, realizing the impact his social media addiction had on his life, knew that he needed to manage his time better. He sat down with Sophia to come up with a plan.

Aniket: "I need your help, Sophia. I know I've been spending way too much time on social media, and it's affecting my studies, my relationships, and my overall well-being."

Sophia: "I know, Aniket. I've been worried about you. But don't worry, I'm here to help."

Aniket: "Thanks, Sophia. So, what do you think I should do?"

Sophia: "Well, first of all, you need to set some boundaries for yourself. Decide on a specific time of day when you'll check your social media, and stick to it."

Aniket: "But what if I miss all the good memes while I'm away?"

Sophia: "Don't worry, the memes will still be there when you get back. Trust me. And besides, it's not healthy to be checking your phone all the time."

Aniket: "You're right, Sophia. I need to be more mindful of my time."

Sophia: "Exactly. And don't forget to schedule in some time for other activities, like studying, spending time with family and friends, and, of course, playing basketball."

Aniket: "You're right, Sophia. I've been neglecting my hobbies and my loved ones because of my social media addiction. I need to make a change."

Sophia: "That's the spirit, Aniket! Remember, balance is key. You don't have to give up social media altogether, but you do need to find a balance that works for you."

Aniket: "Thanks, Sophia. I know I can do this with your help."

Sophia: "Of course, Aniket. I'll always be here to support you."

With Sophia's guidance and support, Aniket managed to successfully implement a schedule for himself. He set specific times of the day when he would check his social media and made sure to schedule in time for other activities such as studying, spending time with friends and family and playing basketball. He also made an effort to be more present and engaged in the activities he was doing instead of constantly checking his phone for notifications.

He also made an effort to engage in activities that he enjoyed that were not related to social media such as reading, going for walks and even picking up a new hobby such as painting.

Aniket also knew that it was important to have people to hold him accountable and remind him to stay on track with his schedule, So he often checked in with Sophia to discuss his progress and address any challenges that he may be facing. Sophia provided a much-needed support system, and Aniket was able to overcome his social media addiction.

Aniket and Sophia also shared a lot of jokes and laughter as they talked about his progress. Sophia often reminded Aniket that it's important to not take things too seriously and to have a sense of humor about things, which helped Aniket to stay motivated and not get discouraged.

Through his journey, Aniket learned the importance of self-awareness, balance, and the power of support from loved ones. He was able to break free from his addiction and lead a more fulfilling life by making sure to manage his time better. He knew that being able to overcome this challenge was a testament to his strength and determination, and that he could face any obstacle that came his way.

As Aniket's habits changed, so did his relationships and perspective. He began to spend more quality time with his friends and family, and found that his relationships with them became stronger and more meaningful. He also found that his focus on academics improved and he was able to achieve higher grades. He also felt more in control and his self-esteem and self-worth improved.

He also began to see the benefits of taking a break from social media and discovered the joys of other activities like reading, painting and going for walks. He found that it helped him to relax and rejuvenate, and it gave him a new perspective on life.

Aniket also became more involved in community service, using his time and energy to give back and make a positive impact in his community. He began volunteering at a local youth center, using his experience and knowledge to mentor underprivileged children and help them to succeed in both academics and sports.

Aniket's story eventually became an inspiration for others, many people reached out to him for advice on how to overcome their own addiction to social media. Aniket would always remind them that change is possible, but it's important to be aware of one's actions, to set limits and most importantly, to have the support of loved ones.

His journey to overcome social media addiction also taught Aniket the value of perseverance and self-control, and how these qualities can help one achieve anything they set their mind to. He became a shining example of how, anyone with determination and hard work, one can overcome any obstacle and come out stronger on the other side. Aniket's story also highlighted the importance of being true to oneself and living a balanced life, where one doesn't let social media or any other distraction consume their whole life.

As Aniket graduated college and started his career, he continued to be an advocate for social media mindfulness and balance, often speaking to students and professionals about his experience, providing advice and encouragement on how to find a balance that works for them. He also continued to be an active volunteer in the community, using his knowledge and skills to inspire and empower others.

Aniket's friendship with Sophia continued to be a major influence in his life, and he always acknowledged her role in helping him overcome his addiction. Sophia was always happy for Aniket's success and was always there to listen and provide support.

Aniket's journey to overcome social media addiction was a long and difficult one, but it also taught him valuable life lessons. He learned that change is possible, and that with the help of loved ones and a strong will, one can overcome any obstacle and achieve great things. He was grateful for the journey and was determined to live a life of balance and fulfillment.

As Aniket grew older, he continued to be known for his quick wit and love of jokes and proverbs. He often used humor and clever sayings as a way to connect with people and to make a point. His favorite proverbs were the old, traditional ones, passed down from generation to generation that carry a deeper message.

Aniket would often start conversations with his friends, family and colleagues by saying something like "A bird in the hand is worth two in the bush." This would catch people off guard but it would quickly break the ice and lead to lively and engaging conversations. He would often use proverbs to make a point, such as "Don't count your chickens before they hatch," to remind people to be patient and not to get ahead of themselves.

His coworkers and friends would often come to him for advice, and Aniket would often use proverbs to provide guidance. "Give a man a fish, and you feed him for a day. Teach a man to fish, and you feed him for a lifetime," was a favorite of his when encouraging someone to take responsibility for their own development, rather than relying on others.

Aniket's love of jokes and proverbs was not limited to just personal conversations, he also used it in his professional life. He would often use them in presentations and meetings to grab attention, lighten the mood and convey his message in a more memorable way. His colleagues would often comment on how his use of humor and proverbs made complex ideas easier to understand and remember.

His unique style of communication, combining his quick wit, love for jokes and proverbs and ability to connect with others, helped him to become an effective communicator and leader. Aniket's use of humor and proverbs also helped to build strong relationships and fostered a positive and productive work environment. His colleagues respected him for his intelligence and his ability to communicate complex ideas in an engaging and relatable way.

Aniket's love for proverbs was also an opportunity to show respect and acknowledge the culture and heritage of his ancestors. The proverbs that he used were a way to keep alive the wisdom and lessons passed down through generations. He believed that these proverbs were a way to connect with one's roots, and to keep alive the tradition and culture of the past. He would often use them as a tool to educate and enlighten others about the importance of preserving cultural heritage.

As Aniket continued to climb the corporate ladder, his love for proverbs and his ability to communicate effectively, helped him to build a successful career. He eventually became a respected leader in his industry and a mentor to many, who looked up to him for guidance and inspiration. He always kept in mind that proverbs, like wisdom, are not owned by anyone, but shared by everyone, and he shared it through his leadership and interactions.

Aniket's unique approach to communication and his love for jokes and proverbs will always be remembered by those who knew him, and his legacy lives on through the wisdom and guidance he shared with others.

As Aniket's success continued to grow, he began to attract the attention of some of his teachers who were envious of his accomplishments. They saw him as a threat to their own status and reputation and began to resent him.

One day, during a class presentation, one of these teachers decided to publicly humiliate Aniket. In front of the entire class, the teacher belittled Aniket, criticizing his work and belittling his achievements. Aniket was caught off guard and was humiliated, feeling embarrassed and ashamed. He felt like he had been stripped of his dignity and self-worth.

After the incident, Aniket felt that he had lost the respect of his classmates and teachers, and that his reputation had been tarnished. He felt betrayed and alone, and struggled to understand why someone would want to hurt him in such a way.

However, despite the negative experience, Aniket didn't lose his spirit and resilience, he continued to work hard and remain focused on his goals. He knew that his success was built on hard work and dedication, and that the envy and jealousy of others couldn't take that away from him.

Aniket's friends, Eric, and Sophia were a great support system for him, they always showed their unwavering support and helped him to see that the words and actions of others don't define who he is. They reminded him that true success is not measured by the approval of others, but by one's own sense of self-worth and self-respect.

Aniket also realized that such incidents are an opportunity for growth, it helped him to become more empathetic, and more understanding of others who might be struggling with similar issues. He also becomes a more determined person and more resilient to negative comments and criticisms. He understood that facing and overcoming such challenges is a fundamental part of personal growth and development.

Aniket decided to use this negative experience as an opportunity to grow and become a better person. He realized that the teacher's actions were not a reflection of his own worth or abilities, but rather a reflection of the teacher's own insecurities and issues. He choose to not to let it affect him and his ambition to succeed.

He also decided to speak up about what had happened, he reached out to the school principal and shared his experience, highlighting the unprofessional behavior of the teacher. The principal took the matter seriously and took steps to address the issue. The teacher was reprimanded for their behavior, and Aniket received an apology for what had happened.

Aniket's strength and resilience in dealing with this situation earned him the respect and admiration of his peers and teachers. He was seen as a role model for standing up for himself and for speaking out against injustice.

As Aniket's story spread throughout the school, he became a beacon of hope and inspiration for others who might be struggling with similar experiences. He showed that it's possible to overcome adversity and to come out stronger on the other side. He also helped to raise awareness about the importance of treating each other with respect and dignity, regardless of their achievements or status.

Aniket's determination and ability to turn a negative experience into an opportunity for growth and learning, not only helped him but also helped others and it also helped to create a more positive and inclusive learning environment for all.

After the incident with the teacher, Aniket was left feeling angry and frustrated. He channeled these emotions into his writing, and began to pen a series of powerful poems about envy and injustice. These poems were a cathartic release for him, as he was able to express his feelings and make sense of what had happened.

Aniket's poems were filled with raw emotion and powerful imagery, as he wrote about the destructive nature of envy and the harm it can cause. He wrote about the feeling of being betrayed and the struggle to regain his self-worth. His poems also spoke about the importance of standing up for oneself and not allowing others to define one's worth or value.

Aniket's poems were widely shared among his peers and teachers, who were moved by his powerful words. His poetry became a voice for many who have been through similar experiences, and it served as a reminder that they are not alone. His poems also helped to raise awareness about the harm that envy can cause, and the importance of treating each other with respect and dignity.

Aniket's poems also reflected his own personal journey, as they expressed his feelings of anger and betrayal and how he overcame those feelings. His poems were not only a reflection of his own experiences, but also served as a source of hope and inspiration for others who might be going through similar struggles.

Aniket's poems became a powerful tool for self-expression and for raising awareness about important social issues. His ability to channel his emotions into powerful words helped him to cope with his own struggles and it helped to empower others to do the same.

One of the poems that Aniket wrote, after he was humiliated by the teacher, was titled "Envy's Poisoned Tongue"

It goes something like this:

> *"Envy's poisoned tongue, a serpent's bite,*
> *A venomous curse, hidden in plain sight.*
> *It whispers lies, it twists the truth,*
> *It steals our joy, it steals our youth.*
> *It clouds our vision, it poisons our mind,*
> *It makes us question, what we hope to find.*
> *It fuels resentment, it breeds disdain,*
> *It tears us apart, it causes pain.*
> *But do not be fooled, do not believe,*
> *The lies that envy, chooses to weave.*
> *For you are strong, and you are true,*
> *And envy's poison, cannot break you.*
> *Stand tall and proud, let your voice be heard,*
> *For you are more, than envy's word.*
> *Let it not define, or bring you low,*
> *For you are the master, of your own flow."*

Aniket's poem, like many others that he wrote, was filled with raw emotions and powerful imagery. It conveyed the destructive nature of envy, the harm it can cause and how it can make a person feel. But it also emphasizes the importance of not allowing envy or others' actions to define one's worth or value. His poem serves as a reminder to always stand up for oneself and not to let envy to cloud judgement or to be swayed by it.

Another poem that Aniket wrote was titled "A Student's Life". It goes something like this:

A student's life, a journey long,
With lessons learned, and songs unsung.
A path of hope, a path of dreams,
A path of growth, or so it seems.
We wear our backpack, and carry on,
Through classes and lectures, and tests at dawn.
We study hard, and work our way,

Through the struggles and triumphs of each day.
We laugh with friends, and make new ones,
We share our dreams, and all our fun.
We learn and grow, as we go on,
A student's life, it has just begun.
We'll make mistakes, and take some falls,
But we'll rise again, and stand tall.
We'll learn from failures, and see success,
A student's life, is one of progress.
So let us strive, and let us learn,
With open hearts, and hearts that yearn.
A student's life, is but a start,
To the journey that will shape our heart.

This poem captures the essence of being a student, the struggles and joys that come with it, and the growth and progress that it brings. Aniket uses imagery of carrying a backpack and walking through classes,tests and lectures as a metaphor for the journey of a student. He emphasizes the importance of making mistakes and learning from them, and encourages to strive for progress and growth. The poem inspires a sense of camaraderie and encourages students to share their struggles, joys, and dreams with one another.

Despite his success, Aniket was not immune to setbacks and disappointments. One such incident occurred during a spelling bee competition where he was representing his class. Aniket had worked hard to prepare for the competition, and had earned a spot in the top two contestants. However, during the final round, the teacher overseeing the competition, named Anand, made an error in scoring, which resulted in Aniket being bumped down to fourth place.

Aniket was shocked and confused by the mistake, and he immediately confronted the teacher, pointing out the error. However, Anand dismissed Aniket's concerns and made the claim that he had simply been lucky to make it that far, and that the competition had been "fair and square." Aniket was furious at this response, and he felt that his hard work and dedication had been dismissed and disrespected.

To make matters worse, the incident was reported in the school newsletter and the news of his finish in the competition was widely spread. Despite his best efforts to clear his name, Aniket became the target of ridicule and jokes from his classmates, many of whom believed that he had been "bumped down" due to luck. Aniket found it hard to shake off the feeling of injustice and felt that his hard work was not recognized.

Aniket found solace in the support of his friends Eric, Sophia, and Sahil Sir, who helped him to see that this incident was not a reflection of his abilities, but rather a reflection of the teacher's poor judgement and lack of professionalism. They encouraged him to speak out and seek justice, reminding him that he deserved to be treated with respect and that his hard work and dedication should be acknowledged.

Despite Aniket's efforts to seek justice and rectify the mistake, the teacher, Anand, refused to admit to any wrongdoing, and the school was unable to rectify the situation. This further compounded Aniket's feelings of injustice and betrayal, and he felt that his hard work and dedication had been dismissed and disrespected.

Aniket found himself struggling to shake off the feeling of unfairness and to move on from the incident. He felt that his reputation had been tarnished, and that he had been wronged by the teacher and the school. He struggled to understand why they had not taken his concerns more seriously, and why they had not done more to rectify the mistake.

Despite the disappointment, Aniket's friends Eric, Sophia, and Sahil Sir stood by him and supported him through this difficult time. They reminded him that he was not alone, and that his hard work and dedication were still valued and respected. They encouraged him to speak out about the incident and to use it as an opportunity to educate others about the importance of treating each other with respect and fairness.

Aniket took their advice, and began to speak out about the incident, sharing his story with others and raising awareness about the importance of treating each other with respect and fairness. He also began to volunteer in the community, using his knowledge and skills to empower others and to advocate for change.

Although the incident was not rectified, Aniket learned valuable lessons about the importance of standing up for oneself and speaking out against injustice. He also learned that even when faced with disappointment and setbacks, it's important to keep fighting for what is right and to never give up on.

Feeling deeply frustrated and helpless, Aniket found solace in writing. He began to express his feelings through shayaris, a form of poetry in Urdu, Hindi language. He wrote about his disappointment, his feelings of injustice and betrayal, and his struggles to come to terms with the teacher's mistake.

Through his shayaris, Aniket was able to process his emotions and make sense of his experiences. His shayaris were filled with raw emotion and powerful imagery, as he wrote about the struggles and disappointments of being wronged and not being heard. His shayari was a form of catharsis for him, and a way to express the complexities of his feelings.

Aniket's shayaris soon spread among his peers and the school community, who were moved by his powerful words and the vulnerability he showed in sharing his story. His poetry became a voice for many who have been through similar experiences, and it served as a reminder that they are not alone.

Some of his shayaris goes like this:

"Jiski koshish ko kabhi na mante,

Woh zindagi ka dushman ban jate"

Which means "Those who never acknowledge your effort, become the enemy of your life."

"Kya karein hum unki nazar ka hai asar,

Jinke liye humne apni zindagi barbad ki"

Which means "What can we do, when affected by their gaze, for whom we ruined our life."

Aniket's shayaris not only helped him cope with his struggles but also helped others to understand and relate to the feeling of injustice and being wronged, it also helped to raise awareness about the importance of treating each other with respect and fairness. His poetry became a powerful tool for self-expression and for raising awareness about important social issues.

As Aniket continued to write and share his shayaris, he began to gain a reputation as a poet, a voice for the voiceless, and a champion for justice. His words resonated with many, who saw themselves in his struggles and felt comforted and empowered by his message of hope and resilience.

Aniket's shayaris became a source of inspiration for many in his community, who saw in him the power to overcome adversity and to create change. His poetry helped to create a sense of community and solidarity, as people came together to support one another in their struggles.

Aniket's shayaris also helped him to come to terms with his experiences, and to find a sense of purpose in his struggles. He realized that even though he was not able to rectify the mistake made by the teacher, his words and actions can make a difference in the lives of others. He found new resolve and determination to use his voice and his talents to make a positive impact in the world.

Aniket's story of standing up for oneself and speaking out against injustice, and his poetry that helped him cope, inspired many, and it showed that one can take something negative and turn it into something positive and meaningful. His poetry became a powerful tool for self-expression and for raising awareness about important social issues, and it serves as a reminder to everyone that everyone has the power to make a difference.

As Aniket continued to grow and mature, he began to think more deeply about the issues he had faced in his own education, and the broader implications of these issues for others who may not have had the support and guidance that he had. He began to realize that his experiences with Eric, Sophia, and Sahil Sir were not the norm, and that many students may not have the same resources and support systems.

Aniket became increasingly aware of the inequalities and injustices that existed within the education system, and he began to question the fairness of a system that privileged some students over others. He realized that his own success was, in part, a result of the support and guidance of his friends and teacher, and that many students may not have the same opportunities or resources.

Aniket also began to recognize that the education system was not just about providing equal opportunities, but also about providing the right kind of opportunities. He realized that the current system often emphasizes rote learning and standardized testing, which may not be the best way for all students to learn and excel. He began to question the system, and think of ways to improve it.

Aniket decided to take action to address the inequalities and injustices he had observed. He began to use his voice to advocate for change and to raise awareness about the importance of providing equal opportunities and support for all students, regardless of their background or circumstances. He also made an effort to mentor and help other students who may not have the same resources and support as he had, in order to help bridge the gap of the unequal opportunities in the education system.

Aniket's reflections and actions on the education system, not only helped him to grow as an individual, but it also helped him to understand the importance of the betterment of the education system for everyone, and how everyone can be a catalyst for change, through mentoring and raising awareness.

Aniket's desire to make a difference in the education system led him to take a proactive approach, He started with taking initiatives to mentor and guide other students who may not have had the same support and guidance that he had. He began to use his own experiences to offer advice, provide resources and encouragement for students who were struggling, he used his skills and knowledge to empower students to achieve their goals, and helped them to build their self-confidence and self-esteem.

Aniket also took a more public approach, by raising awareness about the need for change in the education system, he used various platforms, social media, school assemblies, community events, to raise awareness of the issues and the need for change, and to educate others about the importance of providing equal opportunities and support for all students, regardless of their background or circumstances.

Aniket also began to volunteer in different organizations that focus on improving the education system for underprivileged children, and also using his skills to create resources for children who have limited access to education, such as online classes and resources, to help bridge the gap of the unequal opportunities in the education system.

Aniket's actions and efforts to improve the education system had a profound impact on the lives of many students, and it inspired others to take a similar approach to mentoring and advocacy. He showed that one person can make a difference, and that through mentorship, education and advocacy, it's possible to create a more fair and just education system for all.

As Aniket continued his work to improve the education system, he began to realize that the responsibility for creating a more fair and just system does not fall solely on individual students and teachers, but also on government officials and policymakers. He realized that government policies, funding, and regulations have a significant impact on the opportunities and resources that are available to students, and that in order for real change to occur, the government must also play an active role in creating a more equitable system.

Aniket began to educate himself on the various education policies and regulations, and how they affect the education system, particularly for underprivileged children. He became familiar with the existing laws, policies and programs related to education, and the funding allocated to different education programs and initiatives. He also made an effort to stay informed about new legislation and policy proposals, and their potential impact on the education system.

Aniket began to use his voice to advocate for change in government policies and regulations. He used his platform and his skills to communicate with policymakers and government officials, to educate them about the issues that the students are facing, and to express the importance of investing in and improving the education system, specifically for underprivileged children, who are disproportionately impacted by the inequalities in the system.

Aniket's approach to advocate for change in the education system led him to start discussions and campaigns to create awareness about the importance of the government being responsible for providing equal education opportunities for all, and to seek support from other community members, educators and organizations to lobby for government policies and funding that would improve education for underprivileged children. He understood that a fair and just education system requires investment and commitment from all stakeholders, including the government, and he worked tirelessly to encourage that commitment.

ⵕⵕⵕ

7

Law

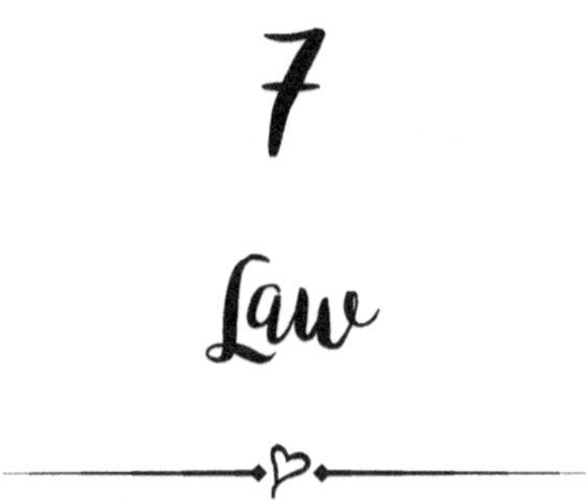

As Aniket's passion for improving the education system grew, he decided that in order to effect real change, he needed to study the law and understand how it could be used to promote education reform.

Determined to take action, he began to research universities and law schools that specialized in education law and policy. He was determined to gain the knowledge and skills necessary to become a legal advocate for education reform.

Throughout his studies, Aniket focused on education law and policy, and how it affects the Indian education system, particularly for underprivileged children. He learned about the various laws and regulations that govern education, and how they can be used to promote equity and access to education for all students. He also studied the impact of funding, policy and curriculum on education outcomes, and how to use data and research to advocate for change.

As Aniket progressed through his legal studies, he also began to think more deeply about the differences between the education systems in India and other countries, particularly the United States. He noticed that the United States and many other countries have standardized tests, such as the SAT and ACT, which are designed to identify talented students and provide them with opportunities for higher education and success.

Aniket began to wonder why India did not have a similar provision in place to identify and support talented students from underprivileged backgrounds. He realized that many talented students in India may not have access to the same opportunities and resources as their peers, and that standardized tests could be a way to level the playing field and provide them with a chance to succeed.

He began to research and educate himself on the impact of standardized tests on education, and how they are used in other countries to identify talented students and provide them with opportunities for higher education and success. He began to use this knowledge to advocate for the implementation of standardized tests in India, as a way to identify and support talented students from underprivileged backgrounds.

Aniket also began to raise awareness about the benefits of standardized tests and their potential impact on education in India. He used his platform and legal skills to communicate with policymakers and government officials, to educate them about the benefits of standardized tests and the importance of providing opportunities for talented students from underprivileged backgrounds to succeed.

Aniket's approach of advocating for standardized test shows that he believes that it can be a way to identify and support talented students from underprivileged backgrounds, which would help in providing the same opportunities for success that many of their wealthier peers have. He also believes that standardized tests could provide an efficient way for the government to identify talented students who could be provided with scholarships, mentorship, and other resources to help them succeed, which would ultimately benefit the society as a whole.

Aniket, upon his graduation from high school, decided to pursue law as a career with the goal of improving the education system in India. He applied to various law schools in India, but ultimately decided to attend the University of Delhi's Faculty of Law, one of the most prestigious law schools in India.

The University of Delhi's Faculty of Law provided him with a comprehensive education in law and the opportunity to gain in-depth knowledge in the field of education law and policy. The program was designed to provide students with a solid foundation in legal theory and practice, as well as specialized courses in various areas of law.

During his studies, Aniket excelled academically and was actively involved in various extracurricular activities, including moot court competitions, debate, and student organizations that focused on education reform. He also took advantage of the university's clinical programs, which allowed him to gain hands-on experience by representing clients in legal cases, under the guidance of experienced attorneys.

Aniket's dedication and hard work during his law school years helped him to gain the knowledge and skills necessary to advocate for education reform. He also gained valuable experience in legal research, writing, and advocacy, which he would later use in his efforts to improve the education system in India.

The faculty members and the university's resources were very helpful for Aniket, in gaining knowledge and expertise, especially in the field of education law and policy, which helped him to achieve his goal of improving the education system in India, and to make a tangible impact in this field.

As Aniket's legal career progressed and he gained more experience in education law and policy, he realized that he had a wealth of knowledge and ideas about how to improve the education system in India. With this knowledge, he decided to write a book that would provide a comprehensive guide to creating an education system that is fair, equitable, and effective for all students.

Aniket began to research and gather information on best practices, successful education systems and policies in other countries, and ways to address the various challenges facing the Indian education system, such as lack of funding and unequal opportunities for underprivileged children. He also began to organize his ideas and thoughts into a cohesive narrative, carefully crafting each chapter to present a clear and compelling argument for educational reform.

Aniket was very secretive about his book, and did not share his plans with anyone. He knew that it would be a monumental task, and he wanted to focus all his attention on the writing and research. He dedicated a lot of his time and energy to this project, working tirelessly to create a book that would have the potential to create real change in the Indian education system.

As he progressed with his book, Aniket realized that writing a book on education reform will be a long-term project, but it also made him more determined to see it through to the end. He saw it as an opportunity to make a lasting impact, not only on the Indian education system, but on the lives of students and families across the country.

Aniket's book would be a comprehensive guide to educational reforms that would explain how an education system should be, and how it can be improved through legal means, and policies that would benefit the underprivileged students the most. It would be a valuable resource for policymakers, educators, and advocates working to create a more fair and just education system in India.

After several months of hard work, Aniket finally completed his book on education reform in India. He titled it "Equality in Education: A Blueprint for Change". The title reflects his belief that the foundation of a fair and effective education system is equality of opportunity, and that the book provides a blueprint for creating such a system.

The book covers a wide range of topics, including the history and current state of the Indian education system, the challenges facing underprivileged students, and the impact of government policies and funding on education outcomes. Aniket also provides an in-depth analysis of the best practices, policies, and programs from other countries that have been successful in improving education for all students.

In the book, Aniket emphasizes the importance of standardized testing as a tool for identifying and supporting talented students from underprivileged backgrounds, and he also provides recommendations for how such tests can be implemented in India. He also suggests ways for the government to invest in and improve the education system, including increasing funding for education programs and initiatives, particularly for underprivileged children.

Aniket also talks about the role of mentorship, counseling and other support systems in helping underprivileged students to succeed, and he explains how such support systems can be implemented in Indian schools and colleges. He also highlights the importance of investing in teachers and providing them with the training and resources they need to support their students' success.

Aniket's book would be considered a valuable resource for educators, policymakers, and advocates working to improve the Indian education system, as it addresses many of the issues that need to be addressed to create a more fair and just system, and offers a comprehensive approach to creating such a system, using legal means and policies that have proven successful in other countries.

Some of the key points that Aniket wrote about in his book "Equality in Education: A Blueprint for Change" include:

1. The importance of equity in education: Aniket stresses that a fair and effective education system is one that provides all students with equal opportunities and resources to succeed, regardless of their background or circumstances.
2. The role of standardized testing: Aniket argues that standardized tests such as the SAT and ACT can be used as a tool to identify and support talented students from underprivileged backgrounds and to provide them with opportunities for higher education and success.
3. The importance of government investment and policies: Aniket highlights the need for increased funding for education programs and initiatives, particularly for underprivileged children, and the need for government policies that promote equity and access to education for all students.

4. The role of mentorship and support systems: Aniket explains the importance of mentorship, counseling, and other support systems in helping underprivileged students succeed, and he offers recommendations for how such support systems can be implemented in Indian schools and colleges.

5. The importance of teacher development: Aniket emphasizes the importance of investing in teachers and providing them with the training and resources they need to support their students' success.

6. International best practices and policies: Aniket provides an in-depth analysis of the best practices, policies, and programs from other countries that have been successful in improving education for all students and how they can be adapted for the Indian education system.

7. The importance of Legal Advocacy: Aniket explained how legal advocacy can play a vital role in bringing change and how to use legal means to improve the education system and bring justice to those students who are marginalized.

In his book "Equality in Education: A Blueprint for Change," Aniket also writes about the importance of incorporating technology in order to improve the education system. Here are a few points that he covers in this area:

1. Identifying students' passions: Aniket suggests that technology can be used to identify students' passions and interests through the use of online assessments and surveys. He argues that by understanding students' interests, educators can tailor their instruction and provide students with opportunities to explore and pursue their passions.

2. Providing practice opportunities: Aniket suggests that technology can be used to provide students with practice opportunities in areas that they are interested in and are passionate about. He suggests that online resources and software can be used to help students develop the skills they

need to succeed in their chosen field.

3. Stipends for passion-based learning: Aniket suggests that technology can be used to provide students with stipends for pursuing their passions and interests. He argues that stipends can be used to help students pay for the costs associated with learning and practicing in their chosen field, such as equipment or materials.

4. Online learning: Aniket suggests that technology can be used to provide students with access to online learning resources, such as e-books, videos, and interactive modules. He argues that these resources can help students learn at their own pace, and that they can be used to supplement traditional classroom instruction.

5. Virtual mentoring: Aniket suggests that technology can be used to provide students with virtual mentoring opportunities. He argues that students can benefit from having access to mentors who are experts in their chosen field, and that virtual mentoring can be done remotely.

6. Virtual internships: Aniket suggests that technology can be used to provide students with virtual internships, which can help them gain real-world experience in their chosen field without the need to travel or leave their own community.

Overall, Aniket's book emphasizes how technology can be used to support students in identifying their passions, provide them opportunities to practice, and provide them with stipends to pursue their passion. He also emphasizes on how technology can be used to support students in developing the skills and knowledge they need to succeed in their chosen field, and to provide access to opportunities for learning, mentorship, and professional development that might not be available otherwise.

In addition to incorporating technology to support students in identifying and pursuing their passions, Aniket also emphasizes the importance of recognizing and encouraging students who excel in certain areas. Here are a few more points that he writes about in this regard:

1. Recognizing exceptional talent: Aniket suggests that educators and policymakers should be proactive in identifying and recognizing students who have exceptional talents and abilities in areas such as science, technology, engineering, mathematics, and the arts. By identifying these students, educators can provide them with opportunities to develop their talents and abilities further.
2. Providing advanced coursework: Aniket suggests that schools should provide advanced coursework and opportunities for students who have exceptional talents and abilities. He argues that by challenging these students with more rigorous coursework, they will be more likely to reach their full potential.
3. Honors and awards: Aniket suggests that schools and organizations should recognize and reward exceptional students through honors and awards. He believes that by recognizing these students, it will encourage others to strive for excellence as well.
4. Special programs: Aniket suggests that schools and organizations should establish special programs for students who have exceptional talents and abilities. These programs could include special classes, clubs, and competitions, as well as opportunities for mentorship and apprenticeship.
5. Encourage Entrepreneurship: Aniket suggests that students who have exceptional talents and abilities should be encouraged to explore entrepreneurship, especially in the field they are passionate about. By providing them with resources and support, they can turn their passion into a business that can benefit not only them but also the society.
6. Scholarships and stipends: Aniket suggests that scholarships and stipends should be provided to exceptional students to help them continue their studies or pursue their passions. He argues that by providing financial assistance to these students, they will be more likely to reach their full potential and make a positive

impact on society.

Aniket's book encourages the children to work hard and explore their talents, he provides them the resources to nurture and showcase their talents, and encourages them to be the change-maker of their own. Through the use of technology and other means, Aniket hopes that children will be provided with the necessary tools, resources and support to excel in their chosen field, to become successful and make a positive impact in the society.

In his book "Equality in Education: A Blueprint for Change," Aniket also writes about the pressure that many Indian families put on their children to pursue traditional careers in fields such as engineering and civil service, and how this pressure can limit children's opportunities and stifle their passions. Here are a few points that he covers in this area:

1. Highlighting alternate career paths: Aniket suggests that families should be made aware of the vast array of career opportunities available to children, including those in fields such as technology, business, and the arts. He argues that by providing children with exposure to a wider range of career options, they will be better equipped to make informed decisions about their future.

2. Promoting entrepreneurship: Aniket suggests that families should be encouraged to view entrepreneurship as a viable and valuable career path, rather than solely focusing on traditional careers. He explains the benefits of entrepreneurship, such as the potential for innovation, creating jobs and the potential for personal and professional growth.

3. Encouraging self-discovery: Aniket suggests that families should encourage children to explore their passions and interests, rather than dictating their career choices. He argues that by allowing children to discover their own passions, they will be more likely to find fulfillment and success in their chosen field.

4. Dispelling stereotypes: Aniket suggests that families should be educated about the ways in which traditional career stereotypes can limit children's opportunities and discourage them from pursuing their passions. He encourages families to challenge these stereotypes and to support their children in pursuing their interests, regardless of whether they align with traditional career expectations.

5. Providing emotional support: Aniket suggests that families should provide emotional support to their children as they make decisions about their future. He encourages families to be understanding of their children's choices, and to provide them with guidance and support as they pursue their passions.

6. Promoting flexibility: Aniket suggests that families should be open to the idea that children's career paths may evolve over time and that it's okay to change one's mind and try something different. He encourages families to promote a culture of lifelong learning and self-discovery, and to support their children in making the most of their talents and abilities, wherever their interests may lead them.

Aniket's book aims to educate the families, as they have a significant role in shaping the future of their children, and to remove the stereotypical approach to career paths, and to provide them with a broader perspective of the opportunities available in different fields, especially in Entrepreneurship.

In his book "Equality in Education: A Blueprint for Change," Aniket also writes about the importance of providing children with freedom and autonomy when it comes to making decisions about their education and future careers. Here are a few points that he covers in this area:

1. Allowing children to make their own decisions: Aniket suggests that children should be given the freedom to make decisions about their education and future careers, rather than having those decisions made for them by their families or society. He

argues that by allowing children to make their own decisions, they will be more likely to find fulfillment and success in their chosen field.

2. Empowering children: Aniket suggests that children should be empowered to take ownership of their education and future careers, rather than being passive recipients of an education system or societal expectations. He encourages parents and educators to give children the resources, support and guidance they need to make informed decisions and to become active agents in their own success.

3. Encouraging creativity and innovation: Aniket suggests that children should be given the freedom to explore their own ideas, to take risks and to think creatively. He encourages parents and educators to provide children with opportunities to experiment, to learn from their mistakes and to develop their own unique talents and abilities.

4. Respecting children's choices: Aniket suggests that children's choices and interests should be respected, regardless of whether they align with traditional expectations or societal norms. He argues that by respecting children's choices, we create an environment where children are free to pursue their passions and to reach their full potential.

5. Creating a culture of autonomy: Aniket suggests that parents and educators should work together to create a culture of autonomy, in which children are encouraged to think independently, to make their own decisions, and to take responsibility for their own education and future careers.

6. Encouraging independent thinking: Aniket suggests that parents and educators should actively encourage independent thinking and critical thinking in children. He argues that these skills are essential for children to be able to make informed decisions about their future and to navigate the world around them effectively.

Aniket's book lays emphasis on the fact that children should be given the freedom to make decisions about their own education and future careers, and that parents and educators should play a supportive role in helping them to develop the skills, resources, and knowledge they need to pursue their passions and reach their full potential. He believes that by providing children with freedom and autonomy, they will be more likely to find fulfillment and success in their chosen field.

In his book "Equality in Education: A Blueprint for Change," Aniket also writes about the negative impact of societal pressure on children and the importance of making it an offense. Here are a few points that he covers in this area:

1. The negative impact of societal pressure: Aniket highlights the negative impact that societal pressure can have on children, including limiting their opportunities and stifling their passions. He argues that societal pressure can cause children to make decisions that are not in line with their true interests and abilities.

2. The importance of legal protection: Aniket suggests that societal pressure should be considered an offense and that legal protection should be provided to children who are subjected to this kind of pressure. He argues that by providing legal protection, children would be more likely to make their own decisions and to pursue their own interests and passions.

3. The role of authorities: Aniket suggests that authorities such as schools, colleges and government should take active steps to combat societal pressure, including implementing policies and procedures to protect children from this kind of pressure, and holding individuals and organizations who exert such pressure accountable for their actions.

4. Advocacy and awareness: Aniket suggests that awareness and advocacy programs should be implemented to educate the society about the negative impact of societal pressure on children and to encourage individuals and organizations to take

an active role in protecting children from this kind of pressure.

5. Protecting the rights of children: Aniket suggests that children's rights should be protected by the legal system and that society should be aware of the same, he encourages legal and non-legal advocacy to fight against this issue.

6. Punishments: Aniket suggests that there should be severe punishments for those who exert societal pressure on children as it can cause severe mental and emotional damage to the children, leading to a lifelong impact on the child's mind.

Aniket's book aims to bring awareness and encourage society to take a stand against societal pressure and make it an offense, providing legal protection and advocating for children's rights. He hopes that by taking a stand against societal pressure, children will be given the freedom and autonomy to pursue their passions and to reach their full potential, free from the constraints imposed by societal expectations.

In his book "Equality in Education: A Blueprint for Change," Aniket also writes about the importance of providing children with a way to voice their grievances and have them addressed by the government. Here are a few points that he covers in this area:

1. Legal Aid Clinics: Aniket suggests that Legal Aid Clinics should be set up in every school to provide children with a safe and confidential way to report societal pressure, harassment, discrimination and other such issues they may face in their schools, to the authorities. These clinics would have lawyers, counselors, and social workers to help children with their complaints and provide them with legal advice.

2. Encouraging children to speak up: Aniket suggests that children should be encouraged to speak up about their grievances and that they should be assured that their complaints will be taken seriously and acted upon. By providing a safe and confidential environment, children would be more likely to come forward and report their concerns.

3. Follow-up actions: Aniket suggests that the authorities should take follow-up actions on the complaints filed by the children and that they should be kept informed of the progress of their complaints. He believes that children's complaints should be taken seriously and that the government should take appropriate actions to address the issues raised.

4. Collaboration with the government: Aniket suggests that the legal aid clinics should work in collaboration with the government to ensure that the grievances of the children are addressed effectively. He believes that the government should take an active role in protecting the rights of children and addressing their grievances.

5. Awareness and education: Aniket suggests that awareness and education programs should be implemented to educate children about their rights and the legal aid clinics available to them. He believes that by educating children about their rights, they would be more likely to speak up when they face problems.

6. Monitoring the effectiveness: Aniket suggests that the government should monitor the effectiveness of the legal aid clinics to ensure that they are meeting the needs of the children and that they are effectively addressing their grievances. He believes that the government should be held accountable for the actions taken to address the issues reported by the children.

Aniket's book suggests that the legal aid clinics would help children to voice out their issues and be heard, it also emphasizes that the government should take actions to address the issues to make sure that children's rights are protected and their grievances are addressed, without any hesitations. He envisions a system where children's rights and well-being are given the utmost priority, where they are protected from societal pressure, and are provided with the freedom and autonomy to pursue their passions and reach their full potential.

In his book "Equality in Education: A Blueprint for Change," Aniket also writes about the importance of primary education and how children should be given the option to focus on their skills while still continuing their studies. Here are a few points that he covers in this area:

1. The importance of primary education: Aniket stresses that primary education up till 8th grade is essential for children's development as it provides them with a strong foundation in language, math, and science. He believes that all children should be given access to high-quality primary education, regardless of their background or circumstances.

2. Skills-based education: Aniket suggests that children should be given the opportunity to focus on developing their skills and talents after primary education. He suggests that this could take the form of vocational training or apprenticeships in fields such as technology, business, and the arts, which would allow children to explore their interests and passions while still continuing their studies.

3. Combination of theory and practical: Aniket suggest that the education system should provide a balance between theoretical education and practical education, children would be exposed to both, they would understand the principles and apply them in real-world scenarios.

4. Personalized education: Aniket suggests that the education system should be more personalized and cater to the needs of individual children, for example, some children might excel in sports, music or dance, the education system should provide opportunities for those children to pursue their passions.

5. Encouraging lifelong learning: Aniket suggests that education should be viewed as a lifelong process and that children should be encouraged to continue learning and developing their skills and knowledge throughout their lives.

6. Curriculum designed for future needs: Aniket suggests that the curriculum should be designed in such a way that it should cater to the future needs and demands of the economy, it should be constantly updated to match the needs of the society.

Aniket's book suggests that primary education is essential for children and should be made accessible to all. He believes that children should be given the opportunity to focus on developing their skills and talents while still continuing their studies, this would allow them to explore their interests and passions while still building a strong foundation in language, math, and science. He also believes that the education system should be more personalized and cater to the needs of individual children, this would lead to the creation of a more efficient and effective education system.

In his book "Equality in Education: A Blueprint for Change," Aniket also writes about the importance of providing facilities and support for dyslexic children in the education system. Here are a few points that he covers in this area:

1. Identifying dyslexia: Aniket suggests that schools should have programs in place to identify dyslexic children and provide them with the support they need. He believes that early identification of dyslexia is critical to ensuring that children receive the appropriate support and accommodations to succeed in school.

2. Appropriate support: Aniket suggests that schools should provide dyslexic children with appropriate support, including specialized teaching methods, assistive technology, and extra time for test-taking and other accommodations. He believes that these supports will help dyslexic children to overcome their learning difficulties and achieve success in school.

3. Inclusive classrooms: Aniket suggests that classrooms should be designed to be inclusive and accommodating to the needs of all children, including dyslexic children. He encourages teachers to use a variety of teaching methods and to incorporate technology and other tools to help dyslexic children to learn.

4. Supportive school culture: Aniket suggests that schools should create a culture of support and understanding around dyslexia. He believes that this will help to reduce the stigmatization that can be associated with dyslexia and will encourage dyslexic children to ask for help when they need it.

5. Parental and community engagement: Aniket suggests that parents and the community should be engaged in the education of dyslexic children. He encourages parents to work with teachers and other professionals to support their child's education and to advocate for their rights.

6. Professional development: Aniket suggests that teachers should receive professional development on how to support dyslexic children. He believes that teachers should be equipped with the knowledge and skills to effectively teach dyslexic children, so they can provide them with the best education.

Aniket's book emphasizes that dyslexia is a common learning difficulty and it is important for education system to recognize the same and provide appropriate support to the children. He argues that by providing appropriate support, including specialized teaching methods and assistive technology, and creating a culture of support and understanding around dyslexia, children with dyslexia will have the opportunity to succeed in school. He also encourages parental and community engagement to support dyslexic children and provide them the best education possible.

In his book "Equality in Education: A Blueprint for Change," Aniket also writes about the importance of giving equal respect to all subjects taught in the education system. Here are a few points that he covers in this area:

Recognizing the importance of all subjects: Aniket suggests that all subjects should be treated as equally important and that students should be encouraged to explore and pursue their interests across a wide range of subjects, not just traditional academic subjects such as math, science, and English.

Valuing diverse fields: Aniket suggest that education system should respect the diversity of fields and not to discourage children from studying a subject just because it is not traditional or highly profitable, but to encourage them to study something which they are passionate about.

Encouraging creativity and critical thinking: Aniket suggests that education should foster creativity and critical thinking, regardless of the subject matter. He believes that this will help children to think independently, question assumptions, and come up with new ideas.

Offering a well-rounded education: Aniket suggests that education system should offer a well-rounded education that exposes students to a wide range of subjects and experiences, so that students can make informed decisions about their future studies and career path.

Allowing for multiple paths to success: Aniket suggests that education system should allow for multiple paths to success, recognizing that students have different strengths, interests and aspirations. He believes that by allowing for multiple paths to success, students will be given the freedom to pursue their passions and reach their full potential.

Providing resources and facilities: Aniket suggest that schools should provide resources and facilities that are necessary to study and explore a subject, he encourages the schools to provide facilities and resources for the diverse range of subjects that are taught.

Aniket's book suggests that education system should give equal respect to all the subjects, recognizing that all subjects are important and have value. He believes that by recognizing the importance of all subjects and fostering creativity and critical thinking, children will be given the freedom to explore their interests, reach their full potential and make informed decisions about their future studies and career path. He encourages the schools to provide resources and facilities for the diverse range of subjects that are taught so that children are able to study and explore their passions.

In his book "Equality in Education: A Blueprint for Change," Aniket also writes about the importance of reconstituting the evaluation system in the education system. Here are a few points that he covers in this area:

1. Re-evaluating the traditional methods of assessment: Aniket suggests that traditional methods of assessment such as multiple-choice tests and standardized exams should be re-evaluated in light of their limitations and biases. He believes that these methods do not accurately measure a student's knowledge and understanding of a subject.
2. Encouraging alternative forms of assessment: Aniket suggests that alternative forms of assessment such as project-based learning, portfolio assessment, and self-assessment should be encouraged and integrated into the education system. These methods provide a more comprehensive and authentic assessment of a student's knowledge and understanding of a subject.
3. Emphasizing on process over product: Aniket suggests that the focus should be on the process of learning, rather than just the final product or outcome. He believes that evaluating a student's progress and understanding of a subject is more important than just their test scores or grades.
4. Providing constructive feedback: Aniket suggests that feedback should be provided to students in a constructive and informative way, rather than just a grade or mark. He believes that this will help students to understand their strengths and weaknesses and improve their performance in the future.
5. Providing opportunities for self-reflection: Aniket suggests that students should be given opportunities for self-reflection and self-assessment. He believes that this will help students to become more self-aware and to take ownership of their learning.
6. Re-evaluating the grading system: Aniket suggests that the traditional grading system should be re-evaluated and a more holistic approach should be used. He believes that this will help to reduce the pressure and stress associated with grades and test scores, and will help students to focus on their learning rather than their grades.

Aniket's book suggests that the education system should reconstitute its evaluation system, re-evaluating the traditional methods of assessment, encouraging alternative forms of assessment, and emphasizing on the process of learning over the final outcome. He believes that this would be more accurate in measuring student's knowledge and understanding and provide students with opportunities for self-reflection and self-assessment, help them to be more self-aware and to take ownership of their learning. It would reduce the pressure and stress associated with grades and test scores, and will help students to focus on their learning rather than their grades.

In his book "Equality in Education: A Blueprint for Change," Aniket also writes about the importance of teachers' professionalism in the education system. Here are a few points that he covers in this area:

1. Emphasizing on teacher education and professional development: Aniket suggests that teachers should be provided with ongoing education and professional development opportunities to improve their teaching skills and to stay up-to-date with the latest research and best practices in education.
2. Encouraging collaboration and sharing of resources among teachers: Aniket suggest that teachers should be encouraged to collaborate and share resources among themselves, this will help to create a culture of professional learning, in which teachers learn from each other and work together to improve their teaching practice.
3. Prioritizing teacher well-being: Aniket suggests that teacher well-being should be prioritized, this includes providing teachers with support and resources to manage the stress and workload associated with teaching.
4. Recognizing and rewarding teacher excellence: Aniket suggests that the education system should recognize and reward excellent teachers by providing them with incentives and opportunities for career advancement.

5. Encouraging teacher autonomy and decision-making: Aniket suggests that teachers should be given autonomy and decision-making power in the classroom. He believes that this will help them to feel more invested in their work and will lead to better results for students.

6. Addressing issues of bias and discrimination: Aniket suggests that the education system should address issues of bias and discrimination in the classroom, including among teachers. He believes that creating a more inclusive and equitable education system requires addressing these issues and empowering teachers to create safe and inclusive learning environments.

Aniket's book suggests that the education system should invest in teacher education and professional development, encourage collaboration and sharing of resources among teachers, prioritize teacher well-being, recognize and reward teacher excellence, and give teacher autonomy and decision-making power. He believes that this will help to create a more effective and efficient education system, where teacher are equipped with the skills and knowledge to provide high-quality instruction and create safe and inclusive learning environments for all students.

Top of Form

Bottom of Form

In his book "Equality in Education: A Blueprint for Change," Aniket also writes about the importance of revising the current reservation system in the education system. He suggests that the current system which has exceeded the 50% limit of reservation set by the constitution should be re-evaluated and modified to better serve the needs of marginalized communities.

Aniket suggests that the reservation should be given only to the economically weaker sections (EWS) of the society rather than caste based reservation. He believes that this will help to address economic inequalities and will provide opportunities for those who truly need it. He suggests that the government should devise a new method to identify the economically weaker sections, this would be more accurate and efficient way to help the marginalized sections of the society and remove the scope of caste-based reservation.

Aniket also suggest that, to ensure that marginalized groups have equal access to education, a system of affirmative action should be implemented to provide targeted support and resources to students from disadvantaged backgrounds, this would be in addition to the EWS reservation. He believes that this will help to level the playing field and ensure that all students have the opportunity to succeed, regardless of their background.

It's important to note that the implementation of reservation policy and its application is a complex and sensitive matter and it would require a detailed study of the current scenario and should be done by considering all the aspects of the society. Aniket's book provides a viewpoint on this topic but it is ultimately up to the government and society to decide on the right course of action.

In his book "Equality in Education: A Blueprint for Change," Aniket also writes about the importance of emphasizing on skills development in the education system. Here are a few points that he covers in this area:

Fostering a culture of skill development: Aniket suggests that education system should foster a culture of skill development, where students are encouraged to develop and refine a variety of skills that are essential for their future career and personal development.

Providing opportunities for hands-on learning and experiential education: Aniket suggests that education system should provide opportunities for hands-on learning and experiential education. This would involve real-world experiences, internships, and apprenticeships to give students a taste of what it's like to work in a particular field and gain practical skills.

Encouraging students to explore their interests and passions: Aniket suggests that education system should encourage students to explore their interests and passions, this would give students the opportunity to learn about subjects that are not typically covered in traditional academic curriculum but that align with their interests and passions.

Emphasizing on soft skills and critical thinking: Aniket suggests that education system should emphasize on soft skills such as communication, problem-solving, and critical thinking skills, which are essential for success in any field and in life.

Incorporating technology and digital skills: Aniket suggests that education system should incorporate technology and digital skills into the curriculum, this would help students to develop the skills they need to thrive in the digital age.

Providing career guidance and counseling: Aniket suggests that education system should provide career guidance and counseling, this would help students to explore their interests and passions, learn about different career options, and make informed decisions about their future.

Aniket's book suggests that education system should emphasis on the skills development, by fostering a culture of skill development, providing opportunities for hands-on learning and experiential education, encouraging students to explore their interests and passions, emphasizing on soft skills and critical thinking, incorporating technology and digital skills and providing career guidance and counseling. He believes that these measures will help students to develop the skills they need to succeed in the future, and will also provide them with the tools they need to achieve their personal and professional goals.

In his book "Equality in Education: A Blueprint for Change," Aniket also writes about the importance of mind games, physical fitness, and mental health in the education system. Here are a few points that he covers in these areas:

1. Mind games: Aniket suggests that education system should include mind games such as puzzles, riddles, and brain teasers as part of the curriculum. These activities help to improve cognitive skills such as memory, attention, and problem-solving.
2. Physical fitness: Aniket suggests that education system should incorporate physical fitness activities such as yoga, gymnastics,

and sports into the curriculum. These activities not only help to improve physical health but also help students to develop discipline, teamwork and leadership skills.

3. Mental health: Aniket suggests that education system should include mental health education as a part of the curriculum. He believes that mental health education is important to raise awareness and reduce the stigmatization of mental illness and that this education should be provided by trained professionals.

4. Incorporating meditation and mindfulness practices: Aniket suggests that education system should incorporate meditation and mindfulness practices to help students to manage stress, anxiety and improve focus.

5. Providing counseling services: Aniket suggests that education system should provide counseling services, this would help students to address mental health issues and to develop strategies for coping with stress and other challenges.

Aniket's book suggests that education system should include mind games, physical fitness, and mental health as a part of the curriculum. He believes that these activities and education would help students to improve cognitive skills, physical health, mental health, discipline, teamwork and leadership skills. This would help students to develop better in all aspects, not just academically but also mentally and physically.

In his book "Equality in Education: A Blueprint for Change," Aniket also writes about the importance of conducting standardized tests in the education system. Here are a few points that he covers in this area:

1. Fair and consistent assessment: Aniket suggests that standardized tests are an important tool for assessing students' knowledge and skills in a fair and consistent way. He believes that standardized tests provide an objective measure of student performance that can be used to compare student achievement across different schools, districts, and states.

2. Identifying areas of improvement: Aniket suggests that standardized tests can be used to identify areas where students need additional support and to guide the development of programs and policies to improve student achievement.

3. measuring the effectiveness of education system: Aniket suggests that standardized tests can be used to measure the effectiveness of education system, by measuring student achievement over time, and comparing student performance to the performance of students in other regions and countries.

4. Encouraging student motivation: Aniket suggests that standardized tests can encourage student motivation by providing them with a clear sense of what they are expected to learn, and by giving them feedback on their progress, so they can see how much they have improved over time.

5. Assessing student readiness for post-secondary education: Aniket suggests that standardized tests can be used to assess student readiness for post-secondary education, by providing colleges and universities with a consistent measure of student performance.

Aniket's book suggests that standardized tests have a important role in education system, it provides fair and consistent assessment, identifies areas of improvement, measures the effectiveness of education system, encourages student motivation and assesses student readiness for post-secondary education. He believes that standardized tests can provide a comprehensive picture of student performance and can help to ensure that students are receiving the high-quality education they need to be successful in their future endeavors.

As Aniket continues to work on his book, "Equality in Education: A Blueprint for Change", he finds himself often reflecting on his own experiences as a student. He remembers the struggles he faced in school, the support he received from friends like Eric and Sophia, and the guidance of his mentor, Sahil Sir. He thinks back to the times when he was lost in the education system and how he found his way through it.

Aniket realizes that many of the ideas he has outlined in his book were shaped by his own experiences and the lessons he learned along the way. He remembers how he was able to overcome his struggles and achieve success through the help of his friends and mentors, and he hopes that his book can provide a roadmap for other students who may be struggling in the education system.

Aniket also thinks about the importance of preserving and nurturing the unique talents of each individual student, and how his own experience as a basketball player taught him the importance of balance and prioritization in life. He looks back with gratitude to the positive impact his friends, teachers and his passion had on his life.

As he nears the completion of his book, Aniket is filled with a sense of purpose and determination. He is determined to use his experiences and the knowledge he has gained to advocate for change and make a difference in the education system, for the betterment of future generations.

Aniket continues to work on his book, but as he delves deeper into the research and writing process, he finds himself becoming increasingly frustrated by the persistence of the same problems in the education system that he had faced years ago. He realizes that despite his best efforts, the education system remains deeply flawed and in need of significant reform.

But Aniket doesn't give up, he continues to work on his book, determined to make it a comprehensive guide for educational reform. He spends many long hours researching the latest educational theories and practices and studying the experiences of other countries with successful education systems. He is determined to produce a well-informed and practical guide that will provide concrete solutions to the problems he has identified.

As he writes, Aniket reflects on the importance of education not just for academic success but for the overall development of an individual, he stresses on the importance of creativity, critical thinking, self-awareness and a sense of purpose which cannot be measured by just grades. He reflects on the role of education in building a just and equitable society and how it can shape the future of the nation.

Aniket's book, "Equality in Education: A Blueprint for Change" is finally complete and he is filled with a sense of accomplishment. He knows that it is not a quick fix for all the issues in the education system but it's a start, a guide that could be used as a tool for change in the right direction. He knows that there is a lot of work ahead, but he is ready to take on the challenge and make a difference in the lives of students, just like himself.

ÞÞÞ

8
Enlightenment through Education: Aniket's Journey of Discovery

———♡———

As Aniket finishes his book and looks back at his journey, he realizes that there is still so much to learn about education and how it can be improved. He becomes curious about different cultures and their way of imparting education, he wants to learn from the best practices from around the world. He begins to feel a sense of restlessness and the desire to seek enlightenment and gain new knowledge.

He decides to take a break from his usual routine and travel to different countries to study their education systems. He visits schools and universities, meets with educators, students, and policymakers to learn about the different approaches they take to education. He becomes fascinated by the diversity of cultures and the ways in which education is implemented.

During his travels, Aniket is struck by the realization that education is not just about imparting knowledge but also about creating an environment that fosters curiosity, creativity, and independent thinking. He becomes convinced that education should empower individuals to think for themselves and make informed decisions.

The experience of traveling and learning from different cultures deepens his understanding of education, and he returns home with a renewed sense of purpose and commitment to his work. Aniket continues to advocate for education reform and he becomes a leading voice in the field, his book becomes a popular and acclaimed publication, his views are sought after by many. He continues to travel and learn from different cultures and is determined to make a positive impact on the education system and society.

As Aniket starts his journey of discovery, he reflects on all that he has gained from his travels and studies. He has gained a deeper understanding of the complexities of the education system and the many factors that contribute to its success or failure.

One of the key insights he gained was the importance of diversity and cultural sensitivity in education. He realized that there is no one-size-fits-all approach to education and that different cultures have different approaches that can be valuable. He learned that by embracing diversity and being open-minded to different perspectives, it is possible to create an education system that is more inclusive and equitable.

Another important insight Aniket gained was the importance of community involvement and collaboration in education. He saw how involving parents, students, educators and policymakers in the education system can lead to better decision-making and more successful outcomes. He also learned that by working together, it is possible to create a sense of shared responsibility for the education system and a commitment to making it the best it can be.

Aniket also gained a greater appreciation for the importance of creativity, critical thinking and independent thinking in education. He realized that a good education system should empower students to think for themselves and make informed decisions, rather than just rote learning.

In summary, Aniket gained a lot from his journey, he gained insight into the importance of cultural sensitivity and diversity, community involvement and collaboration and creativity, critical thinking and independent thinking in education. This has helped him to understand and come up with a more comprehensive approach to education reform. Aniket's newfound understanding and knowledge helped him to further his advocacy in education and make a more impactful change in the education system.

Top of Form

In addition to his travels and studies, Aniket also discovered the benefits of meditation during his journey. He found that meditation helped him to quiet his mind and gain a deeper understanding of himself and the world around him. It helped him to focus on the present moment and to let go of any stress or anxiety he was feeling.

Through meditation, Aniket developed a sense of inner calm and peace. He realized that by taking the time to meditate regularly, he was able to think more clearly, make better decisions and be more productive in his work. He felt that meditation gave him a sense of balance and perspective, which helped him to see things from different angles and to approach challenges with greater insight and understanding.

Meditation also helped Aniket to develop emotional intelligence, by gaining an understanding of his emotions and how to handle them. He learned to recognize and acknowledge his emotions rather than suppress them, this helped him to improve his communication skills and his ability to form and maintain positive relationships.

In his book, Aniket also encourages students to practice meditation as it can help them to handle stress, focus better and improve their overall well-being. He believes that the practice of meditation should be incorporated into the education system as it can have a positive impact on the mental and emotional well-being of students.

In summary, Aniket gained a lot from his journey and he learned that Meditation has great benefits, it helps to quiet the mind and gain a deeper understanding of oneself and the world around, it helped him to focus on the present moment, develop a sense of inner calm and peace, emotional intelligence and be more productive. He encourages students to practice meditation as it can help them to handle stress and focus better.

During his journey, Aniket visited many countries, including Japan, Finland, and Singapore to learn about their education systems. He found that each country had its own unique approach to education and its own set of strengths and weaknesses.

In Japan, Aniket was impressed by the emphasis on discipline, hard work, and perseverance. He was struck by the Japanese saying "Fall seven times, stand up eight" which he found reflected in the students' attitude towards learning. He saw students were able to take their failures in their stride and learn from them, which helped them to develop resilience and determination. He also visited an elementary school and was pleasantly surprised to find that the students were already learning about coding and robotics which he believes gives them an edge in the technological era.

In Finland, Aniket was struck by the focus on equality and the well-being of students. He was impressed by the Finnish saying "The fish swims as well in the small pond as in the big one" meaning everyone can do great things given the right opportunities and resources. He was also struck by the absence of standardized tests and the emphasis on critical thinking and creativity. He also found the Finnish education system gave equal importance to physical activities and mental health which he believes is essential.

In Singapore, Aniket was impressed by the focus on practical learning and the emphasis on math and science. He was struck by the Singaporean proverb "The wealth of a nation is in its children" which he believes reflects the country's commitment to investing in its young people. He was also impressed by the emphasis on developing an entrepreneurial mindset among students.

Aniket found that each country he visited had its own approach to education that was shaped by its culture, history, and values. He also found that each country had its own strengths and weaknesses, and he was able to learn from each of them. Aniket always added a sense of humor and proverbs in his findings and shared them with his friends and family making it easy to remember and made them laugh.

Aniket also visited several other countries during his journey, including South Korea, Germany, and Canada.

In South Korea, Aniket was impressed by the high academic standards and the emphasis on early childhood education. He was struck by the Korean saying "If you want one year of prosperity, grow grain. If you want ten years of prosperity, grow trees. If you want one hundred years of prosperity, grow people." which he believes reflect the importance of investing in the future of its citizens. He also found that the South Korean education system places a strong emphasis on technology and innovation which he believes is an essential part of the future.

In Germany, Aniket was struck by the focus on vocational education and the emphasis on hands-on learning. He was impressed by the German saying "A good beginning is half the battle" which he believes reflects the importance of starting a task well. He also found that the German education system has a well-structured apprenticeship system which help students to gain real-world experience and become employable.

In Canada, Aniket was impressed by the focus on multiculturalism and the emphasis on language education. He was struck by the Canadian saying "A stitch in time saves nine" which he believes reflects the importance of taking care of small problems before they become bigger ones. He also found that the Canadian education system values and recognizes the diversity of its student population and encourages the preservation of each student's culture and language.

Aniket's journey was full of learning and new experiences.

During his journey, Aniket was fortunate enough to have the opportunity to meet some of the great personalities in the field of education. One such person was Dr. A.P.J. Abdul Kalam, the former President of India who was known as the "Missile Man of India" for his work in the field of missile technology.

Aniket met Dr. Kalam during his visit to India. Aniket was quite excited to meet Dr. Kalam and was a bit nervous too. But as soon as he met Dr. Kalam, he felt quite comfortable with him. Dr. Kalam asked Aniket about his book and Aniket told him about the journey he took to write the book and the points he had mentioned in it. Dr. Kalam listened to Aniket attentively and then said, "My young friend, education is not just about getting good marks and degrees, it is about developing a strong character and a good heart." Aniket felt quite inspired by these words.

Another great personality Aniket met was Former President of United States of America Mr. Barack Obama. Aniket was thrilled to meet Mr Obama, he couldn't believe his luck. Mr Obama was impressed by Aniket's book and its contents. Aniket jokingly said " Mr President, looks like you have a serious competition for your book" Mr Obama laughed and replied "Never underestimate the power of a young mind to change the world, keep doing what you are doing, It takes courage to change the system."

Aniket was quite taken aback by the words of these two great personalities, he felt that their words would be his guiding light in his journey. He also felt quite humbled by the fact that these great personalities took the time to speak with him and offer their encouragement. Aniket left these meetings with a renewed sense of purpose and determination to make a positive impact on the education system.

Aniket also had the opportunity to meet some other great personalities during his journey. One of them was Sir Ken Robinson, the world-renowned education expert, and author. Sir Ken Robinson is known for his work on creativity, innovation, and education. Aniket was excited to meet him and discuss his book. They had a conversation about the points Aniket has mentioned in his book, and Sir Ken Robinson praised Aniket's ideas and encouraged him to continue his work. He said "Aniket, You have a great idea, keep working on it. The world needs more people like you who are willing to challenge the status quo and work towards creating a better education system for all."

Aniket also met with Malala Yousafzai, the youngest Nobel Prize laureate, who is known for her work in promoting education for girls. Aniket was inspired by her story and her courage, and they discussed the importance of education and the challenges that girls still face in accessing education in many parts of the world. Malala said " Aniket, education is a powerful tool that can change the world, it's important to fight for the right of every child to have access to education. I wish you all the best with your book and your work."

Aniket also met with the Founder and CEO of Khan Academy, Salman Khan, who is known for his online education platform and his work to make education accessible to all. They discussed how technology can be used to improve education and make it more accessible to all. Salman Khan said "Aniket, technology can be a powerful tool for education, and I am glad to see that you are thinking about how to use it to improve the education system."

Aniket met these great personalities and learned a lot from them. He also realized that all of them has a common goal of improving the education system and that it is achievable with the right approach and mindset. He also found it was fun and entertaining as he was able to crack jokes and use proverbs to make the conversations more lively.

As Aniket's journey of exploring and learning about different education systems came to an end, he found that his journey of personal growth and self-discovery had just begun. Along his journey, Aniket met many people, he made many friends, and he discovered many new things about himself. Among all the people, he met, one person stood out. Her name was Megha, she was a fellow traveler who shared a common interest with Aniket in education reform.

Aniket and Megha had many conversations on the different education systems and how they can be improved. They had many debates and many laughs together. They both found that they had a lot in common, and they enjoyed each other's company. Aniket was drawn to Megha's passion and dedication to making a positive change in the education system. Megha was impressed by Aniket's creativity and his ability to think outside the box.

As time passed by, Aniket realized that he had developed feelings for Megha. He knew that he wanted to spend the rest of his life with her. He decided to tell Megha about his feelings. Megha felt the same way and was happy to hear that Aniket felt the same way about her. They both knew that they wanted to spend their lives together, working towards the common goal of improving the education system.

Aniket and Megha decided to get married and continue their journey of education reform together. They found that they were able to achieve more together than they ever could alone. They started a movement to make education accessible to all children and to provide equal opportunities to all. They worked together to make education more interesting, interactive and accessible to everyone.

As they say "When two people meet who are capable of understanding each other, half of the world's troubles are over." This was the case with Aniket and Megha. They found a partner in each other who understood them and supported them in their mission. Aniket finally found the person who was with him in the journey to change the education system and also found the partner with whom he could share the joys and sorrows of life.

Aniket and Megha's conversations and jokes were always filled with wit, humor, and wisdom. They both had a great sense of humor and they would often use jokes and proverbs to lighten the mood and to make their conversations more interesting. Their conversations were not limited to education reform, they talked about a variety of things and they found that they shared many common interests.

One of their favorite jokes was about a math teacher who was always grumpy and would always yell at his students. Aniket would say "Why was the math teacher always angry? Because he had too many problems." Megha would reply "Why don't mathematicians ever get any rest? Because they are always solving problems."

Another one of their favorite jokes was about a science teacher who was always talking about experiments. Aniket would say "Why did the science teacher love experiments? Because it was always a test in life." Megha would reply "Why did the science teacher always wear goggles? So he could see the results of his experiments."

Aniket and Megha also liked to use proverbs in their conversations. Aniket would often say "Give a man a fish and you feed him for a day; teach a man to fish and you feed him for a lifetime" to stress the importance of providing education to people so they can be self-sufficient. Megha would often say "You can't make an omelette without breaking eggs" to stress the importance of taking risks in order to achieve one's goals.

Their jokes and conversations always reflected the light-hearted side of the education reform, it also helped them to bond better and form a deeper connection with each other. They found that laughter and humor are essential to enjoying life and achieving one's goals. They also realized that their ability to make each other laugh is an important part of the foundation of their relationship.

As Aniket and Megha continued their journey of education reform, they came across many people who had a similar interest in making a positive change in the education system. One such person was Aniket's old friend, Eric. Aniket had not seen Eric in many years, they had lost touch after they finished school. But, one day, Aniket received a call from Eric, he was working in a software company and was back in the city.

Aniket was thrilled to hear from Eric and they immediately set up a meeting. When Aniket met Eric, he was surprised to see how much Eric had changed. He was now a successful software engineer and had a great job at a reputed company. Aniket was happy for Eric and they talked about old times and caught up on everything that had happened since they last saw each other.

Eric was curious about Aniket's work on education reform and he asked Aniket about his book. Aniket told Eric about the journey he had taken to write the book and the points he had mentioned in it. Eric was impressed by Aniket's work and he offered to help Aniket in any way he could.

Aniket was happy to hear this, he knew that Eric's expertise in technology could be a great asset to his book and he accepted Eric's offer. Together they came up with an idea of using technology to improve the education system and make it more accessible to all children. They made a plan to develop an interactive learning platform that would provide equal opportunities to all children and help to identify their talents and passions.

Aniket and Eric's friendship was strengthened by this shared interest, and Eric was happy to reconnect with his old friend and to be able to contribute to Aniket's work. They both joked that "A friend in need is a friend indeed" and both felt fortunate to have each other in their lives.

As Aniket and Megha continued their journey of education reform, they decided to visit the United States to explore the education system there and to see how it could be improved. During their visit, they met many people who were working to make a positive change in the education system. They were impressed by the level of innovation and technology that was being used to improve education in the US.

One of the people they met was a man named Jack, who was a school teacher in a rural area. Jack was dedicated to providing his students with the best education possible, despite the limited resources available to him. He used technology to enhance his students' learning experience, and he had a unique approach to teaching which was unconventional but very effective. Aniket and Megha were impressed by Jack's approach and they learned a lot from him.

They also met a woman named Jane, who was a college professor and had a wealth of knowledge about higher education. She shared her insights about the education system in the US and the challenges that college students face. Aniket and Megha appreciated the different perspective Jane provided and she introduced them to the American perspective on Education system.

They also met a group of young entrepreneurs who had started an education-based non-profit organization to help underprivileged children. They were inspired by the passion and dedication of these young people, and they were impressed by the impact they were making on the lives of children in need. They had a lot of fun with them as they went out exploring and Aniket and Megha loved the way these young entrepreneurs cracked jokes to make the environment lighthearted.

Aniket and Megha were grateful for the opportunity to meet such amazing people, who were working towards a common goal of improving the education system. They found that by sharing ideas and collaborating, they were able to achieve much more than they ever could alone. They came to the realization that "A journey of a thousand miles begins with a single step", they took the first step in their journey to change the education system and now they were surrounded by people who had similar goals and would support them in the journey.

As Aniket and Megha continued their journey of education reform, Aniket started to reflect on his own passions and interests. He realized that in his focus on education reform, he had let go of some of the things that he loved to do. One of those things was writing shayaris. Aniket had always been passionate about shayaris, it was a way for him to express his thoughts and feelings in a poetic way.

Aniket shared his realization with Megha, and she encouraged him to start writing shayaris again. She reminded him that it was important to have passions and interests outside of work, and that it would be beneficial to him both personally and professionally. Aniket took Megha's advice and started writing shayaris again.

He wrote shayaris about the struggles and joys of education reform, about the beauty of nature, and about love and friendship. His shayaris were full of emotion and wisdom, and they resonated with many people who read them.

Aniket started to share his shayaris on social media, and they quickly gained popularity. People were impressed by the depth of his poetry and the insights he provided. Aniket was encouraged by the positive response and it helped him to rejuvenate his passion for writing shayaris.

As Aniket continued to write shayaris, he started to gain recognition in the world of literature. His shayaris were featured in magazines and newspapers, and he was invited to speak at events and festivals. Aniket was humbled by the recognition and it was an important step in his journey as a writer.

Aniket realized that passion and interests should not be neglected and should be nurtured. He joked with Megha " A passion is like a flower, when it blooms it's a delight to the senses and when it withers, it's a source of regret". Writing shayaris was a source of delight for Aniket and he was happy to have rejuvenated it.

Here are a few examples of shayaris Aniket had written:

- "Har chirag andhere mein jalta hai, Magar roshni sirf unhi ke kaam aati hai, Jo apni hawa mein chirag jalate hain" (Translation: Every light shines in darkness, But only those who kindle the light in themselves, Succeed in spreading light around.)
- "Sach kehte hain log, Koshish karne walon ki haar nahi hoti, Magar koshish karne se pehle, Jeet ki zid karne ki zaroorat hai" (Translation: It's said that those who try, do not lose, but before trying, one must have the determination to win.)
-
- "Har sawal ka jawab nahi hota, Har armaan pura nahi hota, Magar jo dhang se koshish karte hain, Unke liye kamyabi ka rasta dikhta hai" (Translation: Not every question has an answer, not every desire is fulfilled, But those who try in the right way, find success on their path.)
- "Zindagi ek chunauti hai, Jo har kisi ke liye alag hai, Magar jo zindagi se takra jate hain, Unhe zindagi jeet jati hai" (Translation: Life is a challenge, different for everyone, But those who face life head on, emerge victorious)

As Aniket continued his work in education reform and writing shayaris, he also made time for travel. He and Megha travelled to many different places, both in India and abroad, to gain new perspectives and to find inspiration for their work.

They visited many beautiful places in India, from the snow-capped peaks of the Himalayas to the lush green forests of the Western Ghats. They explored ancient temples and forts, and learned about India's rich cultural heritage. They also enjoyed meeting new people and learning about their way of life.

Aniket and Megha also visited many countries abroad. They explored the bustling cities of Europe, the pristine beaches of South East Asia, the ancient ruins of Latin America, and the breathtaking landscapes of Africa. They loved trying new foods, learning new languages, and experiencing different cultures. They found it interesting to see how different countries have different approaches in education and how it has helped them develop.

Aniket and Megha also enjoyed many outdoor activities like trekking, skiing, and camping. They loved the feeling of being surrounded by nature, and they found that it helped them to clear their minds and to find new inspiration for their work.

The couple always found some time for themselves and enjoyed exploring the night life, food, and different cultures that each country had to offer. They also loved to take pictures to remember the beautiful memories. They always had a great time together, always joking and laughing and for Aniket travelling was an opportunity to take a break and come back to work more revitalized.

Aniket realized that travelling not only helps one to learn about new cultures and places but also learn about themselves, their strength and weaknesses and how to adapt to new environment.

As Aniket continued to grow in his personal and professional life, he always kept his sense of humor and love of proverbs close at hand. He found that they helped him to put things in perspective and to find the positive in any situation.

Aniket always had a good joke ready to lighten the mood, whether he was in a meeting with government officials or discussing an issue with colleagues. He found that jokes helped to break the ice and to build connections with people.

Aniket also loved to use proverbs to make a point or to add wisdom to a conversation. He had a vast collection of proverbs, both from India and from around the world, and he always had one that was just right for the occasion. He had an ability to remember them all and to use them correctly.

As Aniket became more successful in his work, he didn't forget his humble beginnings. He always remembered the struggles he had faced, and he used jokes and proverbs to keep himself grounded. He believed that "Kamzor ki himmat, majboot ki taaqat hoti hai" (Translation: The courage of the weak is the strength of the strong).

Aniket also took the opportunity to teach and share his jokes and proverbs with the young students who he mentored. He found that they were a great way to connect with them and to help them to see things in a new way. He enjoyed the looks on their faces when they understood the meaning of a proverb or when they got a joke and laughed.

Aniket's passion for education reform, his love for shayaris, his travels, and his jokes and proverbs all contributed to the person he had grown to be. He had a unique perspective on the world, and he used it to make a positive impact on the lives of those around him.

Despite his success, Aniket never lost touch with his roots or forgot where he came from. He remained humble and grounded, always remembering the struggles he had faced in his own life.

One way Aniket stayed grounded was by staying in touch with his old friends, Eric and Sophia. He would often call or visit them, and they would reminisce about the old days. Aniket would tell them about his work and his travels, and they would tell him about their own lives. These conversations helped Aniket to stay connected to his past and to stay grounded in the present.

Aniket also made a point to give back to the community. He would often return to his old neighborhood and volunteer at the local schools. He would help out with classes, run sports clinics, and be a mentor to young students. Through these volunteer efforts, Aniket saw firsthand the struggles that many people still face, and it reminded him of his own struggles. He felt that it kept him grounded and empathetic.

Aniket was also conscious of the privileges he had been fortunate enough to have, like a great teacher and supportive friends, which allowed him to be successful. He knew that not everyone had the same opportunities and that there was still a lot of work to be done in the field of education. This kept him motivated to keep working towards change and improvement in the education system, rather than getting complacent with his own achievements.

Aniket's humility and grounded nature also extended to his personal life. Even though he had achieved success and had a comfortable life, he lived simply and avoided flashy and ostentatious displays of wealth. He believed in the value of hard work and perseverance, and he lived by the maxim "simple living, high thinking."

Aniket remained the same person who had a passion for basketball, shayaris, jokes, and proverbs, but his experiences had taught him the value of humility and groundedness. He never forgot where he came from, and it helped him to continue to make a positive impact on the world.

Aniket was deeply inspired by the late President of India, Dr. APJ Abdul Kalam. He had met him during his travels and had been struck by Kalam's humility, wisdom, and dedication to the people of India.

Aniket was impressed by Kalam's vision for India as a developed nation, where people have equal opportunities, and where everyone has access to quality education. He was inspired by Kalam's belief that "Dream, dream, dream. Dreams transform into thoughts and thoughts result in action." He felt that Kalam's message was in sync with his own beliefs on how the education system should be like.

Aniket was also inspired by Kalam's emphasis on the importance of scientific and technological education. He felt that this was an essential aspect of education reform and something that could greatly benefit the people of India. He was also influenced by the way Kalam promoted a culture of innovation, creativity, and entrepreneurship in the young students, which he had learned during his conversations with the former president.

Aniket was struck by Kalam's humility and his dedication to serving the people of India. He found that Kalam's message of selfless service, humility and hard work resonated with him on a deep level, and he felt a strong connection to him. He felt that Kalam's message was universal and that it could apply to anyone, anywhere.

Aniket was deeply saddened when Kalam passed away and felt a personal loss. He felt that Kalam's life and legacy had a profound impact on him and he felt a deep sense of gratitude for the time he had spent in Kalam's company. He felt that Kalam had been a mentor and an inspiration to him, and he felt a deep sense of responsibility to carry on Kalam's message to the world.

Aniket's encounter with Kalam deeply influenced him and it strengthened his resolve to work towards the betterment of the education system, to uplift the youth and to realize his own dream of a developed nation, where everyone can reach their full potential.

Aniket took the inspiration he gained from Kalam and channeled it into his work as an advocate for education reform. He wrote his book, which he had been working on, on education reform and it was published, He named it "Vidya Ka Aviskar" (Innovation of Education) to pay homage to Kalam, as he felt that the former president had always been an advocate for innovation in education.

In his book, Aniket proposed several solutions to improve the education system, such as the use of technology to test students' passion and provide them with hands-on experience, providing stipends, and encouraging children to explore their interests and talents. He also proposed solutions to increase the participation of children from economically and socially disadvantaged backgrounds.

Aniket also spoke at various conferences, seminars, and events, sharing his insights and experiences, and advocating for education reform. He would often quote Kalam's words, such as "Learning gives creativity, Creativity leads to thinking, Thinking provides knowledge, and Knowledge makes you great" to emphasize the importance of education and the role it plays in personal and societal development.

Aniket also started a non-profit organization, with the name "Dr APJ Abdul Kalam Institute" in the memory of his inspiration, which works on the betterment of education system and the upliftment of underprivileged children. He felt that it was important to give back to the community, just as Kalam had done, and to make sure that everyone had access to quality education, regardless of their background.

In short, Aniket's encounter with Kalam had a profound impact on him and shaped his worldview. He felt that Kalam's message of humility, hard work, and selfless service was something that he could apply to his own life and work. He felt that Kalam's legacy would continue to inspire him in his endeavors and he made it his life's mission to carry on Kalam's message of innovation, creativity and working for the betterment of society through education.

Aniket's non-profit organization soon gained momentum and support, he started to establish the "Dr APJ Abdul Kalam Institute" in various parts of the country with the main aim of promoting education and innovation in the field of education. The organization began to work on various projects that aimed to improve the education system by providing resources and support to underprivileged children, providing free education and extracurricular activities, as well as providing scholarships and stipends to talented students from underprivileged backgrounds.

Aniket also began to work with various other organizations and educational institutions to promote education reform and to raise awareness about the importance of education. He collaborated with teachers, policymakers, and other education experts to create programs that would provide students with the resources and support they needed to succeed.

Aniket's organization also focused on providing mentorship opportunities for students and providing resources for career development. He created a program that connected students with professionals in the field of their interest, providing guidance and resources that helped students to reach their full potential.

Aniket also began to receive recognition for his work, he was invited to several universities in India and abroad as a guest speaker to share his insights and experiences in the field of education reform. He had a strong message for the students, about how one can make a positive impact in the world by working towards a common goal, and how the right kind of education can make all the difference.

Aniket's story is a testament to the power of education, hard work, and perseverance. His journey from a poor student to an education reformer is an inspiration to many and has changed the lives of thousands of students. His work continues to have a positive impact on the education system and it will always be remembered as a shining example of how education has the power to change lives.

As Aniket's organization continued to grow and make a difference in the education system, Aniket himself grew as a person as well. He learned to be more empathetic and understanding towards the plight of underprivileged children and began to see education as a right, not a privilege. He would often say that "if you want to change the world, you must first change the education system, and if you want to change the education system, you must change the way we think about it."

Aniket also began to appreciate the value of self-care and self-improvement. He realized that in order to make a positive impact on the world, he needed to first take care of himself. He began to meditate and practice yoga regularly, which helped him to develop a more peaceful and centered mindset.

As he delved deeper into his interest in poetry and literature, he found solace in the written word and used it to express his feelings and thoughts in a more meaningful way. He started to write Shayaris and poems more often, as a way to channel his emotions and connect with others. He had a blog where he writes shayaris, poems and thoughts, it gained a good number of readers. He would often say, "Poetry is a mirror that reflects the world and our place in it."

Aniket's dedication to education reform and his work with the Dr APJ Abdul Kalam Institute continued to inspire many. He received several awards and honors for his work, and his book "Vidya Ka Aviskar" became a best seller. His organization, the Dr APJ Abdul Kalam Institute, continues to make a difference in the lives of thousands of children across the country.

In conclusion, Aniket's journey from a poor student to an education reformer is a testament to the power of education and hard work. He had faced many obstacles along the way, but he never gave up. His work with the Dr APJ Abdul Kalam Institute and his book "Vidya Ka Aviskar" have made a lasting impact on the education system, and his story will continue to inspire generations to come.

ϷϷϷ

9
The Implementation

As Aniket's passion for education reform and his work with the Dr APJ Abdul Kalam Institute continued to flourish, he decided to take it one step further by running for a political office in the hopes of bringing about larger-scale change in the education system. With the support of his friends, family, and organization, he campaigned tirelessly and managed to secure a seat as a Member of Parliament.

As a Member of Parliament, Aniket took his knowledge and experience and used it to advocate for education reform on a national level. He proposed several bills and policies aimed at improving the education system, including increased funding for schools and educational resources, implementing standardised tests, and increasing support and opportunities for students from underprivileged backgrounds.

He also started to work with the government to implement the points he mentioned in his book, "Vidya Ka Aviskar" and also "Equality in Education: A Blueprint for Change" such as using technology for the betterment of education, skills development, and to provide resources for children with special needs. He also worked towards the implementation of the 'National Education Talent Search Examination' which was aimed at finding talents from all over the country, regardless of their background.

He also pushed for the government to bring about stricter laws against societal pressure and child labor, ensuring that every child has the right to education and the freedom to choose their career paths. Aniket's hard work and dedication began to bear fruit as many of his proposed policies and bills were passed and implemented.

Aniket's work as a Member of Parliament brought about real change in the education system. His efforts helped to increase enrollment in schools, improve the quality of education, and provide more opportunities for students from underprivileged backgrounds. He became a role model for many, particularly for those who had been told they couldn't achieve their dreams because of their background, He had a message to all of them, "never give up on your dreams, as with hard work, dedication, and the right opportunities, anything is possible."

As Aniket took office as a Member of Parliament, he quickly set to work on the proposals and ideas outlined in his book, "Equality in Education: A Blueprint for Change". With his extensive knowledge and experience in the field of education reform, he was able to navigate the complex political landscape and bring about real change in the education system.

Aniket's efforts to improve the education system were nothing short of revolutionary. He proposed major amendments to the constitution, leading to the formation of a national education talent search examination and providing equal opportunities and resources to children from all backgrounds. He also worked towards the implementation of policies that would provide education and support to children with special needs and dyslexia, and pushed for the government to bring about stricter laws against societal pressure and child labor.

As a result of his tireless efforts, India's education system underwent a significant transformation. Enrollment in schools increased, the quality of education improved, and students from underprivileged backgrounds were provided with more opportunities than ever before. Aniket's work was hailed as a triumph, and he became known as "the second Ambedkar" for his contributions to education reform.

Aniket's efforts also brought about greater equality in education, breaking down the barriers that had held back students from underprivileged backgrounds for so long. His proposals and policies helped to level the playing field and provide every student with the opportunity to succeed.

His work also helped in India becoming a superpower, as the country had a highly educated population that was equipped to meet the demands of a rapidly-evolving world. His work in the education system was instrumental in driving India's economic and technological advancements, as well as fostering greater social cohesion and harmony.

Aniket's legacy lives on as a beacon of hope and inspiration for all those who believe in the power of education to change lives and shape the future.

Aniket's tireless efforts did not stop with just bringing about changes in the education system. He also worked towards the betterment of the society in general. He became the driving force behind several initiatives aimed at uplifting the underprivileged and underrepresented communities.

He advocated for policies that provided more job opportunities, better living conditions and healthcare for the people living in rural and backward areas. He brought attention to the issues facing the marginalized communities and pushed for their rights to be respected and protected.

He also became an advocate for clean energy and sustainable development. Aniket's vision of a greener future helped to lead India on a path towards becoming a world leader in the transition to renewable energy and reducing the country's carbon footprint.

Aniket's work towards the betterment of the society made him one of the most popular and respected leaders in the country. He was widely seen as a true leader who had the interests of the people at heart, and who was dedicated to creating a more just and equitable society for all.

As his term as a Member of Parliament came to an end, Aniket's work was widely recognized and celebrated. He received numerous awards and honors for his contributions to education reform and social justice. He became an inspiration for many and a role model for future leaders to emulate.

Aniket's legacy continues to live on, through his books, his policies, his initiatives, and the countless lives he has changed and inspired. He had left behind a strong foundation for future generations to build upon, and his work will be remembered as one of the most remarkable contributions to the Indian society and Education system.

Aniket's work in education and social justice also helped to inspire a new generation of leaders and activists, many of whom followed in his footsteps to continue the work he had begun. His vision for a more just and equitable society was embraced by many, and his ideas and policies were widely adopted by other politicians and leaders.

With the support of the new generation of leaders, the work Aniket had begun to continue to flourish, leading to even more significant changes and improvements in the society and education system. His writings, speeches and policies were studied in universities and schools as it became a handbook for many who wanted to work towards a better India.

As Aniket grew older, he remained active in public life, continuing to advocate for education and social justice. He traveled the country, giving speeches and sharing his experiences and insights with others. He wrote several more books, sharing his knowledge and wisdom with future generations.

Aniket's life and work had a profound impact on India and the world. His contributions to education and social justice were widely recognized and celebrated, and his legacy lives on through the countless lives he has changed and inspired. He will always be remembered as a true leader and a shining example of what one person can accomplish when they are driven by a desire to make a positive change in the world.

As Aniket's vision and work gained more and more recognition, he was invited to speak at various international conferences and forums on education and social justice. His ideas were adopted by other countries and his reputation as a visionary and leader in the field grew on a global level. He was invited as a keynote speaker to many countries, sharing his insights and experiences with leaders from all over the world.

Aniket's work also gained him recognition from international organizations working for the betterment of education and human rights. He was awarded several prestigious awards and accolades for his contributions to the field.

Aniket's work had a wide-reaching impact, not only in India, but also around the world. He was seen as a global leader in education reform and social justice, and his legacy continues to inspire others to work towards creating a more just and equitable society for all.

Aniket's work also led to India becoming a leader in education and human rights. The country's education system was considered one of the best in the world and its citizens were highly educated and skilled. The country also became a leader in the field of human rights and was often looked up to as an example by other countries.

In his later years, Aniket continued to be active and engaged with the society. He dedicated much of his time to mentoring the young leaders and helping them to continue his work. He passed away in his late 80s, but his legacy continues to live on through his work and the many lives he has touched.

Overall Aniket's life was an exceptional journey, an epitome of excellence and an inspiration for many to come. It was a story of hard work, determination and perseverance that led him to become one of the most respected and celebrated leaders in India.

When Aniket passed away, his wife discovered a collection of poems that he had written throughout his life. They were a reflection of his thoughts, feelings, and experiences. Many of the poems were about his journey in life, the struggles he faced, and the lessons he had learned.

There were also poems about the issues he had fought for throughout his life, such as education reform, social justice, and human rights. These poems captured the passion and intensity of his beliefs and the depth of his commitment to making a positive change in the world.

There were also poems about love, relationships, and the beauty of nature, which reflected Aniket's appreciation for the simple things in life. They were a reminder of the importance of finding joy and meaning in everyday experiences, even amidst the struggles and challenges of life.

Aniket's wife decided to publish a book of these poems, with the title "The Poetry of Aniket: A Legacy of Inspiration" . The book became a bestseller and was widely read and appreciated by people from all walks of life. It was considered a fitting tribute to Aniket's life and work, and a powerful reminder of the impact that one person can have when they are driven by a deep sense of purpose and a desire to make a positive change in the world.

Aniket's poetry was widely celebrated, many young poets found inspiration in his works, several schools used his poetry to inculcate good values in children. It was Aniket's another way of leaving an indelible impression on the society and his fans.

Overall, the book was considered a treasure trove of wisdom and inspiration, an enduring legacy of a great leader and a true humanist. It continued to inspire generations to come to work towards building a better society and a more just world.

Some of his works is as follows:

A Life, Well Lived

"A journey of purpose, a heart full of fire,

Aniket walked through life, with a burning desire,

To change the world, to make it a better place,

With every step, he set a steady pace.

Through trials and tribulations, he fought with might,

For education and justice, day and night,

With a pen as his sword and a book as his shield,

He battled for a future that was fair and yield.

He faced many challenges, and his resolve was strong,

He pushed through the struggles, and he pressed on,

His passion for change, a beacon of hope,

He inspired others, and they began to cope.

With his leadership, he brought forth change,

And the country's education, he did re-arrange,

A true visionary, a leader of note,

Aniket's legacy will forever float.

He shared his wisdom, in poetry and prose,

His words of inspiration, will forever compose,

Aniket's journey, a story to be told,

Of a life well-lived, with purpose and bold.

A shining example, of what one can be,

When driven by a desire, to make a difference, for humanity.

🐦🐦🐦

"

Acknowledgements

This book began as a big, messy thing and required something more than just my own hand to chisel something comprehensible out of it.

As a child, I became aware of the injustices present in the education system and decided to take action. I began researching and writing about the challenges faced by marginalized students and the educators and advocates working to bring about change. Through extensive research and personal anecdotes, I was able to provide valuable insights into the systemic issues that perpetuate educational disparities and offer practical solutions for achieving educational justice.

Moreover, I could not forget to give the credits to:

Notion Press: Publisher

Komal Kamra: Publishing Manager

& Most of all, My Mother and Father